Love Makes All The Difference...

About A Puppy

You should adop a puppy from the animal shelter. A puppy whoud be a good pet. Puppies are cute, funny and Sweet. A Puppy can jump, fetch and do tricks Puppies will play with you, love you and be your friend. You should adopt a Puppy from the animal shelter because They love you so much and they need a new home.

by Emma Reed

8 years old
Lumpkin County Elementary School

Paw Prints
On My Heart

Stories, poems, drawings and photographs
celebrating homeless animals
who found love and hope

Contributed by members and friends of
PAWS Humane Society
Dahlonega, Georgia

Edited by Deborah Smith

About A Puppy

Pets Need A home
You Should a dopt a Pet from the
animal shelter. A PUPPYY would be
a good Pet. PUPPies are cute,
Playful, and soft. PUPPies can
give Riss, JUMP, and do tricks.
PUPPies will Love you, sleep with
You, and be your friend. You Should
a dopt a PUPPY from The animal
shelter because it is cute and Louely.

Love bul.
     BY Brooklyn Wimpy

7 years old
Lumpkin County Elementary School

Pet **A**doption and **W**elfare **S**ociety, Inc.

Acknowledgements

PAWS, with generous assistance of local veterinarians, provides low cost spay/neuter services to those in our community who cannot afford it. All proceeds of this book will be used to fund this service.

PAWS Dahlonega no longer works directly with our county shelter because those efforts fail to solve the underlying problem of too many animals. We have chosen to focus on humane education and spay/neuter as the best way to permanently protect all pets in our community and reduce the number of homeless animals that end up in a shelter.

Caring, proactive veterinarians in our community reduce their charges for spay/neuter services when a PAWS voucher is used. Applications for the PAWS Spay and Neuter Assistance Program (SNAP) voucher are widely available from merchants and assistance agencies throughout our community. Updated contact information is provided on our website: pawsdahlonega.com

PAWS Humane Education Program promotes responsible pet ownership with spay and neuter as the central tenet of our message.

Please join in thanking our local best-selling author, Deb Smith, who made this book possible. Deb and her husband, Hank, approached us with the idea of doing a book as a fundraiser. They edited and published the book for us, and are contributing all profits from PAW Prints on My Heart to the PAWS spay/neuter program.

PAWS Dahlonega's efforts are possible due to the generosity of Dahlonega veterinarians, those who contributed their heartfelt pet stories for the book, those who purchase PAW Prints on My Heart, our publishers Deb and Hank Smith and to all who contribute to and support our spay/neuter efforts.

We hope you enjoy our stories and encourage you to contact us and give us your feedback.

Tell us which stories you liked and send us your own pet stories for future editions. You can find information about submitting stories and comments on our web site: **pawsdahlonega.com**

See PAWS Dahlonega on Facebook for updates, lost and found, and pets needing a home.

We thank you,
PAWS Board of Directors

Bebe uses these soulful eyes to get whatever she wants . . . and it works. My husband and I brought her home from a local shelter as a two-months-old pup. Now she's a big, galloping, tailwagging "friend" to six patient cats and one older dog, all of which were rescues like her.

—Deborah Smith, editor
PAW Prints on My Heart

Paw Prints On My Heart

Contributed by members and friends of

PAWS Humane Society
Dahlonega, Georgia

PAW PRINTS ON MY HEART
Print ISBN: 978-1478228134
© COPYRIGHT PAWS HUMANE SOCIETY 2012
Disclaimer: All contributors to PAW PRINTS ON MY HEART gave permission for their work to be published for this non-profit, fundraising book, with all profits going to spay and neuter programs for pets.
Cover images and other PAWS photos by permission
White horse art (page 124): © Avarito @Dreamstime

If your pet could talk, what would it say?
Thank you to the students of Mrs. Dicken's 2nd Grade.

Contents

Did You Ever Notice ...

Susan S. Dodds

- People remember pets' names better than their owners' names.

- Sometimes you might call your children by one of your pet's names or vice versa.

- Even when your memory starts to fade, you never forget pets you have had.

- Smiling to yourself when you remember pets from your past and their impact on your life.

- How excited a dog gets when his/her owner returns home.
- How petting a cat or dog makes you forget or put aside your problems and even smile when you are sad.
- How a purr or a lick can make you feel better.
- How loved you feel when you have something warm and furry snuggle up to you.
- How those big brown eyes looking up at you can melt your heart.
- How dogs smile when they are happy.
- How cats get lovey and rub against your legs when they want something.
- How pets will tease each other like kids do.
- How cats, like some humans, have selective hearing.
- How your pet often understands your emotions.
- How a soft purr or a wagging tail can lift the weight of the world from your shoulders.

I'm Your Huckleberry!

Vicki Truelove

On Monday December 5th, at eleven sixteen p.m., Vicki, who heads up the Georgia Division of The Dog Liberator, (TDL) posted on Facebook a dog that she wanted to rescue. I was in bed! Our TDL team went into action, and it was quite remarkable. We didn't know the shelter, their protocols, or the true status of this dog; yet there was something about this dog that made everyone excited. The post indicated that he was scheduled for euthanasia on December 6th, at eight thirty a.m.. Can you rescue a dog overnight? I think the answer is yes!
—*Giselle, founder of The Dog Liberator*

Here's what Vicki wrote the evening of December 6th:

Last night was one of those nights. One of those nights in rescue when furry faces are pleading with you from your computer. My heart was aching, stomach churning, fingers typing furiously trying to arrange rescue for dogs in a Georgia High Kill Shelter that were slated to be put down this morning. We are rescue volunteers working together for the sake of these fur-babies.

One in particular stood out to me. His picture wasn't a good one, but you could still see the confusion in his eyes. I took one last look at this boy, referred to as #116043, and hoped someone would save him. It was three a.m. I needed sleep. Maria the Marvelous is a volunteer rescue coordinator for the shelter that I had never met before. I knew she was working tirelessly to get as many dogs as possible out of the shelter, if she was sending messages past three a.m. She wanted me to call her in the morning. I was to pick up a dog for her from a vet near me, and she was going to get #116043 for me. Then we would meet and swap dogs.

When I called her, I woke her up. She was upset that she had overslept, and had little time to get to the shelter to help the rescuers get dogs out. This shelter does not hold dogs, so you have to be there by eight thirty a.m. If you are not there, once the vet arrives, it's over.

From the moment I spoke with her that morning, I knew I had to hurry, no time, leave nothing to chance . . .

I was racing against time with heavy morning traffic, rain, and the fear I wouldn't make it. Yelling at my GPS which had sent me 'round and 'round the long way, wishing I knew the roads better. Maria called to tell me that the shelter knew I was on my way, but there are no guarantees. I was almost there, when Maria called again and said she was leaving the shelter, the vet was there to do her job. Maria needed to leave, but promised to wait and beg for #116043.

I was slowing at a red-light when I got Maria's call, I was one block away. As her words rang in my ear, my foot stepped on the gas. I ran the light just as it turned. I couldn't take the chance, the chance that one red-light would make me too late.

When I arrived, the office was silent. The staff looked at me and said they were sorry but it was too late. Well, anyone that knows me knows that I never take no for an answer.

An animal control officer was standing at the door to the kennels, I could see the anguish on his face. I begged, showed him my info, and pleaded nicely. I could tell by the look on his face that he thought #116043 was already gone. But all of a sudden he said "I'll try," and rushed through the door to the back of the shelter, which he was not allowed to enter while the vet was putting dogs down.

The officer was gone for a while . . . I waited. Another officer told me that he was the one that picked up #116043. "He was chasing tail!" He explained. "In hot pursuit of a female dog, trying to be her Huckleberry!"

Finally, the first officer appeared, and handed me a card. "You can have him," and he smiled. Then he disappeared into the back again. I was elated. So were the other officers. "He's a gorgeous dog, very sweet," one officer said.

The officer in charge came back in the room. He began to tell me that a lady claiming to be #116043's owner, had come to claim him. "It was odd," he said. When she went to the kennel, instead of the dog greeting her with happiness, he went to the back and sat down. There was no excitement or acknowledgement for his lost owner. When the lady went to sign the paperwork and was told she would have to pay to retrieve him and get him neutered, she balked. Eventually she left, leaving him to fate.

The officer said, "If she was his owner, she wasn't who he was waiting for. It's as if he was waiting for someone else to come for him. He hasn't eaten since he got here. He just sits quietly. It's as if he'd rather be here at the shelter than go home with his owner."

Finally, they said #116043 was ready. I went to wait outside at the gate. As the officer was walking him to me, I noticed blood on his front leg. I looked at the officer and he at me. "What happened?" I asked. "Nervous, chewed his leg because he knew what was going on. Dogs know," he said.

When I looked closely at his leg I knew that it was not nervous chewing. It was blood on his leg from a needle stick. My suspicion was confirmed when I noticed that he was very groggy.

When I tried to get him to jump into the car, he laid down and hugged the ground. I petted him, held him and talked to him for a bit.

He was waiting on me and I was almost too late.
He was one second away from the Rainbow Bridge.
The kind and caring officer helped me get him in the

car. #116043 sat quietly in the seat, looking at me with those beautiful eyes. "I am so sorry baby, so sorry you had to go through that, but I'm here now and you are going to be okay. We will find you a home that loves and appreciates you," I assured him.

The Officer in charge is a wonderful man. He is a former dog trainer who loves and appreciates dogs. #116043 and I will be forever grateful for his compassion. Just this once, he said yes, and stopped euthanasia that had already begun.

First Freedom Ride

#116043 and I went straight to the vet for a health check. I looked closely at his collar, and noticed that the clasp had been broken. Someone, possibly his former owner, had simply tied the collar in a knot. A sickening feeling came over me. The broken collar itself represented lack of care, and if you can't take the time to replace a collar, you won't take the time to give your dog heartworm preventative. I had never rescued a heartworm positive dog before, but I knew this one would test positive. Everything added up that this dog was not valued. I shook my head in disbelief, but held my head high knowing that today is the first day of his new life. "You're a TDL dog now, head up, be proud, never again."

#116043 marched right into the vet's office, and greeted everyone, including a sick cat. He climbed right up on the scale and weighed in at 64.4 lbs. He was a little thin but overall in good shape. I asked for a heartworm test, expecting the answer would be positive, and it was. The vet recommended the slow but very safe treatment for heartworm and I agreed.

Anita the Amazing, a TDL volunteer who had been online helping facilitate this rescue, called me and offered to pay for boarding #116043 while we arranged foster care and transport. When I told her I was at the vet and his HW status was positive, she paid for medications and the HW test.

#116043 I'm your Huckleberry!

As the vet continued her examination, the dog leaned his head against her and nuzzled her. When we left, there were several dogs coming in for boarding. #116043 wagged his tail and was very polite. This time, he jumped in the car on his own, first wanting to drive, and finally relinquishing the seat after I explained to him that he didn't have a license.

The rest of the day he politely rode with me. We went through Starbucks and all the workers came to the window to see him and commented on what a beautiful dog he was. He didn't seem to let it go to his head. I offered him water and ever so politely he drank from the bowl as if he was being careful not to spill. While I was driving, he watched out the window as if he knew where he was going.

I sent a text message to TDL foster mom, Erin Pippin, with #116043's picture. Can you foster for a few days? He's in my car. She said yes! We arranged a meeting, and even though Erin was working on her thesis for an MBA and expecting family to visit for her upcoming graduation, she still said, "yes!"

Throughout the day, Anita called to check our progress. She was on the phone with me when everyone in Starbucks was going gaga over him. Foster family members, Kevin and Sam, were posting and messaging trying to find out if #116043 made it. They both offered to foster and help transport him from Georgia to Florida. As all of this was happening, #116043 was very calm, and I know why, he knew that he had the best, biggest-hearted rescuers on his side, and there was simply nothing to worry about.

Erin with #116043

We pulled up to Erin's place and #116043 hopped out. He said hello, and saw Erin's female dog, Lucy. His eyes lit up and he went into his manly posture, wagged his bushy tail, and strutted around to impress her. He's a real ladies man!

As I started to leave, he walked toward me, and looked me in the eyes. I waved him back to his cushion in front of the fireplace. That's the last time I saw him, next to Erin's pretty Christmas tree on his cushion. His eyes had joy and he appeared to be smiling. I told him I loved him and this was just one step on the magnificent journey that lies ahead for him.

I had climbed back in my car for another two hour drive when the emotions of the day consumed me. I was so happy he was safe, so horrified at how close we had come to losing him, so thankful for Anita, Erin, Sam, and Kevin for their part in his rescue, and grateful that I met Gisele and joined The Dog Liberator team.

Gisele and I had met months ago when our paths

crossed because of a homeless dog. Without that fortuitous meeting, I would not have had the opportunity to know such wonderful, giving people who made it possible for us to rescue twenty dogs that day. Sometimes passion overtakes us, I cried and said a prayer for those dogs that didn't have anyone coming for them. I realized long ago that I must focus on those I can save. I am also aware that animal control officers and the shelter staff do not create this problem.

#116043 is a classic example. He had not been neutered; so he wandered off whenever a lovely female went into season. His owner had not taken responsibility for him, would not spend 65 dollars to retrieve him, and left him to an uncertain fate.

I asked Gisele if I could name him Huckleberry, and her answer was "yes!"

The notice we posted:

Adopt Huckleberry and give him a warm bed, a Christmas tree to sit under, and a stocking filled with love. He's worth it. Look into those big, brown eyes and tell him "You're home" and watch his eyes twinkle and a smile cross his face as he says. "I know, I'm your Huckleberry!"

Foster Update Dec. 9:

Erin reports that Huckleberry is a love. He is house trained, not a single mistake since he's been there. He can Sit, Lay Down, and Shake. Her dogs love him and he loves them back. What a wonderful loving dog someone just threw away! Huckleberry has happily settled in.

Tomorrow Huckleberry starts the next leg of his journey. He will be transported to Florida to foster with Sam who had been on the internet that night trying to save him. She anxiously awaits the moment she can put her arms around Huckleberry. Once in Florida, Huck's next trip should be to a forever home that will make all the effort worthwhile. Vicki's

ADOPT Huckleberry story on our blog produced 900 hits in one day, 7,000 in a week! We received more response and applications to adopt Huck than we had ever received for any dog. We all have received emails and posts from people who were unaware that this kind of thing goes on in our shelters.

Our biggest task was wading through the applications to decide who got to take this wonderful boy home.

Huckleberry now has a wonderful family who takes him everywhere . . . soccer practice, bike riding, playing twister! He has started heartworm treatment and is doing well. He is living his fairytale, happily ever after.

Now I still shed tears for my Huckleberry, but they are tears of joy for this sweet boy and his wonderful new life!

The following pictures are Huckleberry today. Alive, loved, and a blessing to his family.

Rescued by Vicki Truelove and The Dog Liberator Rescue

That beautiful face, no longer worried.

See next page for more —>

Being loved on
and spoiled.

Sitting pretty.

Playing twister with the
girls at Christmas.

Hemmingway

By Phyllis Ellis

An old orange tabby cat
Who cannot hear
Walks the back yard
Without any fear.
The dogs in the neighborhood
Stay away from our yard
For Hemmingway is a six toed cat
And knows how to guard.
Hemmingway stands his ground
If a dog should be at bay
And shows his mighty twelve claws
And says "Stay away!"

If your pet could talk, what would it say?
Thank you to the students of
Mrs. Dicken's 2nd Grade.

Jocy

Emily Lewy

The afternoon Jocy was turned in at the animal shelter I was sitting in the waiting room. She was an absolutely adorable ten month old puppy with shiny black fur, short legs and a very large head. I later learned that she was a retriever mix.

Her owner was giving her up. At forty pounds, she was not the little puppy that the owner had originally adopted.

Jocy was in excellent condition, so we began to take her out each Saturday in hopes of finding a new home for her. She was not used to a leash, but she learned quickly. Many people admired her. Such an affectionate and well-mannered dog, yet, no one chose to adopt her.

After almost three weeks with no one interested, we were concerned for her future. The shelter was full with more animals coming in each day. Dan, our PAWS member who arranged transfers of shelter pets to rescue organizations, asked me to foster Jocy.

At first, I refused. My husband would not want more than the two dogs and two cats we already had. I was concerned about how she would get along with cats; and then, my dogs might not like her.

So, my friend Sandy and I took her out for adoption

again. Once more, no takers. There was no way Jocy could spend more time in the shelter. Such a wonderful dog!

Taking her home with me was to be an experiment. Would my husband become attached to Jocy quickly enough that we would be able to keep her? How would the other pets react to her?

I snuck her into the shower before anyone knew she was there. She should at least smell like the other dogs!

Oh, you should have seen Jocy run into the back yard! She was so excited to be able to run free. She raced around with the other dogs having the best time. Then she dived into the fish pond. Jocy got two more baths that day because she kept diving into the pond. Barriers had to be placed around the pond until she learned that the pond was not her space.

When Sandy came by to see us, my husband explained to her that we were only fostering Jocy. Sandy winked at me. We both realized that he was beginning to appreciate the new member of our family.

And of course we adopted her. There was no way our Jocy could go back to a shelter. She snuggles up with the other dogs on the sofa. She sleeps with us on the bed. 'Walking the dogs' now means walking three, not two. We make a lot more trips to the pet food store. And the house needs a lot more cleaning.

Jocy has a forever home with a family who loves her passionately.

What I Learned from a Possum

Erin Peck

When I was volunteering at a wildlife preserve several years ago, someone brought in a baby opossum. It was found beside the road where its mother had been hit and killed by a passing automobile. We figured it was probably about ten weeks old, since it was able to eat on its own instead of still having to nurse.

The owner of the preserve said that in another month it would be old enough to survive on its own but that it would need looking after in the meantime. He asked me if I would take on the responsibility. I hesitated at first, looking down at that ugly little creature with its repulsive naked tail. My love of all animals, especially babies, finally overcame my feelings of revulsion about caring for—of all creatures!—a 'possum. I named him Peter O'Possum because his long, angular face reminded me of Peter O'Toole.

I didn't really spend much time with Peter at first, only touching him when I had to take him out of his cage to clean it. He was so small that I could hold him with one hand. After a few days I realized that he never made any

effort to bite me; instead he kept trying to snuggle up to my neck.

I had always thought of 'possums as rather nasty creatures. However, Peter was meticulous about grooming himself and kept himself cleaner than my cats did. It was obvious that he did need some help with his long tail, which dragged on the ground when he walked, so I cleaned it regularly with baby wipes.

Then one day it happened. I looked into Peter's jet black eyes, and he looked back at me without blinking or looking away as most animals will do when you make eye contact with them. How can I describe the feeling I experienced? I can only say that it felt like pure love flowing between us.

I started spending more time with Peter, often letting him out of his cage. He followed me wherever I went, and if I stopped, he promptly sat on my feet and started licking them. If I squatted down, he nuzzled and groomed me wherever he could reach. When we sat on the couch, he loved to lie on his back in the crook of my arm and go to sleep with his little pink tongue sticking out. Every day Peter and I would look into each other's eyes and rekindle that feeling of love and absolute trust.

What I learned from Peter O'Possum is not to judge by exterior appearances but to look for the inner beauty that exists in all creatures. When I first saw him, my past conditioning about 'possums told me that he was repulsive. A few days later I had fallen in love with this adorable little animal.

I don't know if opossums are capable of loving as we humans understand the concept of love. However, the trust he showed in me and the affection he expressed by nuzzling and grooming me made me feel loved by him. I know that I loved him, and 1 still think of him often and treasure the memory of the time we had together.

When I find myself having negative thoughts or starting to be judgmental about the way others look or act, I remember Peter and I remind myself to look for the inner beauty and goodness that I believe exists in all of us even when we are not aware of it. Who knows? Perhaps by seeing it, we help to draw it forth into expression.

Rudy's Story

Cathy Sanford

My name is Cathy Sanford. My pet's name is Rudy. Rudy is a six and a half year old Yorkshire Terrier who weighs three pounds and seven ounces. Rudy worked as a pet therapy dog for a little over five years before retiring in January 2012.

Rudy loved to visit the nursing home, hospital as well as participate in the READ program at the library. Rudy always looked forward to his monthly visits, especially having the kids read to him. He has his own chair and became so relaxed that he would shut his eyes during the session and dream he was in the story. The Pet Therapy program was very rewarding to both Rudy and his owner.

Rudy also loves to swim and jump off the diving board. Rudy makes sure he wears his life jacket to keep safe. Rudy's favorite hobby is riding motorcycles and he has his own helmet, goggles, leather vest and tie. Rudy loves to feel the wind blowing in his hair.

Rudy is sending in a picture of himself ready to ride. Rudy also loves to have his picture taken.

No stranger has ever been known to put their hand in 2-b's truck window.

6-23-09
nmk

Going Home
Ivana Pelnar-Zaiko

I'm scared. Gone is the warmth, gone is mother's den,
So unfamiliar, black and cold these bars!
Can't run, can't see but walls or closest pen.
Last loving snuggle? Can't remember when . . .

What now? Some voices, doors slamming on cars—
The sounds and smells, the memories rushing in:
Hands full of kindness . . . or inflicting scars.
Which ones are near, what's for me in the stars?

The cage is opened, human reaches in,
I cannot hide, run, duck or disappear!
But he caresses, pets, scratches my chin.
I hear a young voice, "Daddy, I want him!"

Dare I to hope? May cuddle, love be near?
I look into a friendly face, a broad smile,
Another, girl's face I need not fear,
And lady, boy—both grinning ear to ear.

Please stay and choose me! Don't move down the aisle!
I lick their faces, jump and run and wag,
On one goal focused all my puppy guile:
"Please take me home, and not just for a while!"

I'm leashed but can't stop now, I pull and drag,
Oh bliss! The family brings me home this day.
I'm given toys, play tugging on a rag,
They pick my name, affix a silver tag.

The children feed me, hours spend in play,
I know this home is heaven—and it's mine!
They pet and hug me, and I know I'll stay,
"My heart is yours!" I so wish I could say.

"The toys make stronger teeth, to chew them's fine,"
I'm told; but what's the difference from that shoe
And something called clean laundry on a line
To tug on, or on which to try to dine?

I hide from their raised voices. Wish I knew
Why they don't walk me anymore. What crime
Was so severe that anger, scolding grew
Until I'm lonely more and more, anew.

The boy and girl lost interest in time,
The parents tied me in the yard outside.
There's so much love still in this heart of mine!
I bark it night and day, come rain or shine.

When neighbors shouted, "We will get your hide!"
They took me to the place where prison lay.
I whined and shivered all along the ride,
Pup memories flooding all my grown-up pride.

They said good-bye, but why, I couldn't say.
The shelter staff were kind and let me bay my sorrow.
I heard "He has another day to play!"
Oh, good! Forever home awaits! Tomorrow!

Shayla Shar Pei

Charlene Johnson

Sit! .... I said 'Sit!'

Mama, I am sitting.

Shayla. Why do I have to repeat myself? I should only have to tell you ONE TIME—not over and over again.

But I'm sitting now. Doesn't that count for something?

Oh, you're nothing but a hound dog!

A hound dog?

Yes, a COON hound dog.

But, you said I was Shar Pei.

Down! ... I said 'DOWN!' ... DOWN SHAY!

Okay, but you don't have to yell. You know I heard you the first time. My hearing is exceptional, you know.

Except for those little, bitty ears, you're hearing is pretty good. You look like a brindle colored pound puppy. I remember when I first found you on the internet. What a beautiful blend of cinnamon with black stripes.

I must take after my mama. What did she look like?

I'll never know, so I guess you'll never know either. Somebody dropped you off in a cardboard box with three of your sisters at the front doors of the dog pound. You were only about six weeks old.

Why would they do that?

I can only imagine. ... I've never seen a stray Shar Pei.

Judging by the wrinkles you had, your mama was probably Shar Pei. She must have been in heat and somehow she was unescorted in the yard. You know, male dogs can smell a female in heat for miles and miles. They just can't help themselves. And they are willing to travel the distance to mate with the female.

So who do you think my daddy was?

Well, they tell me that your sisters didn't look like you at all. One was all white and the others were black. You were the only brindle. So I imagine several males mated with your mama. The ad said you were a Boxer mix and that's part of the reason I wanted you. I already had a Shar Pei/German Shepherd and I thought you'd be a great companion for Oscar.

So I'm a Boxer?

That's the strange part. After driving all the way from Atlanta to Cedartown to pick you up, (the drive took a couple of hours), the papers said you were Shar Pei / German Shepherd. I remember the groomer who was re-homing you saying "Who changed the papers? This is not a Shepherd!'

So which one was I—Boxer or Shepherd?'

That's the interesting part. Your head was HUGE so I though the Boxer part was right, but you just didn't act like a Boxer.

How so?

A lot of Boxers are pretty laid back. And they aren't known for being terribly nose-driven. You were always sniffing something.

So?

And then you started digging up the yard. I had more holes in the yard than a little bit. And I mean DEEP holes. Sometimes the holes were more than a foot and a half deep! Hound Dog!

Hey! No need for name calling!

I recently went to a local dog show and saw dogs that looked just like you, except for the ears - the same cinnamon brindle marking, a speck of white on the chest, dramatically black eyeliner setting off a black muzzle.

Hey, that sounds like a Plott Coon Hound.

You guessed it. A typical Shar Pei mix will have the markings and body of the mix and the head of the Shar Pei.

Including the ears?

Yep, including the ears and the mindset. That explains

why you have such short cute little ears.

But I can still hunt?

Yep.

And I can still track?

Yep.

And I can still guard? I got that from my mama's side of the family.

Yep.

So I'm still a great dog?

Yep.

And you're still gonna let me stay here with you?

Wouldn't have it any other way.

And you're still gonna be my forever mama?

Yep. ... I wouldn't trade you for all the pedigrees in the world. You're fun, well-mannered and a Canine Good Citizen. Gotta respect the pound puppies of the world. You ROCK!

A Home

Tiffany Welshans

I rest my furry paws on the cold concrete floor
And wait and wait and then wait some more.
I am surrounded by others of my kind
Who bark and beg to be played with.
They scream out,
"Don't forget about me!"
I reassure them that no one will,
But even I myself am unsure of that.
There are so many animals here,
Each with their own story,
And they all seem very open about their past lives.
The pampered poodle with wiry white fur
Once belonged to a prestigious family
Who groomed her daily and put red ribbons
In her fur.
The cocker spaniel belonged to a little girl,
I believe her name was Natalie,
Who was sweet and silly and smart;
The cocker spaniel would lie at the end of the girl's bed
And warm her freezing feet during the winter.
Even the boxer would talk about his long runs on the
    beach
With his master at his side;
He would often fetch Frisbees in the park

And chase a bouncing ball.
Some of us will not talk about the past.
There once arrived a basset hound
Who was as silent as the calm before a storm.
She would not speak nor lift her head,
But I saw it.
Across her left eye was a scar,
And her body was bloody and bruised.
She would whimper at night,
Begging for someone to hold her
And tell her that the world is not as wicked as she thinks.
She left soon after coming;
Where she went I know not.
I, too, cannot wait to escape my cage
And have the sun smile on my face again.
I long to roll in God's green grass,
And like a puppy who first opens his eyes,
I would look at the world with wonder and
Explore everything I encounter.
I long for a family to adopt me-
A dog in his prime who is not afraid to learn new tricks.
I do not care to live in a nice house;
I just want a home.
I have continued to wait and wait.
I have seen the poodle go, the cocker spaniel and boxer
　　leave,
Countless puppies go to loving families,
But yet I continue to wait.
It might not be possible, but maybe, just maybe,
I wait and continue to wait for
You.

An Unappreciated Gift

Susan S. Dodds

When my husband and I were newlyweds forty seven years ago, we lived in an apartment building a block from a large city university. My husband worked the late night shift and I was home alone. Having grown up with cats and dogs, that was the one thing missing in married life. Our apartment building had a NO PETS policy. The landlady and her husband lived on the first floor directly under our apartment. During hot summer evenings while studying at our kitchen table, I would sometimes put the chain lock on the door to the outside porch and leave the door open a crack to get fresh air.

One night while deep in my reading, I heard a familiar sound . . . a meow! I looked up just in time to see a scrawny little gray and white cat slip through the opening of my door. I immediately jumped up to pet him, but he wanted no part of that! Some fresh milk and a piece of my hamburger from supper made a big hit with him and he purred loudly as he lapped his milk. Knowing that pets were a "no, no" and that my husband had been raised with dogs and did not particularly like cats, I made sure that the little guy was out of the apartment. I always closed the door before my husband arrived home from work at midnight.

The cat and I held a secret rendezvous every night for about a month. He began to let me pet and even hold him at times . . . always in exchange for milk and meat. He cooperated with me about leaving before the stroke of midnight. I did not even attempt to name him because I knew it was impossible to keep him. I was thrilled just looking forward to his brief visits.

One night the cat did not come at his usual time. I kept watching the clock and hoping he would come. I eventually fell asleep on the couch, but forgot to close the door to the porch. Some noise awakened me. As I stretched and yawned, I noticed that I had forgotten to close the door and take the chain lock off so my husband could come in when he arrived home. Looking at the clock, I saw that he was due home in about thirty minutes. As I started back to the couch to lie down I saw a movement out of the corner of my eye. My friend, the cat, had decided to visit after all . . . and he had brought me a present.

The cat started toward me making a strange guttural sound. Hanging out both sides of his mouth was a squirming, squealing rat! I screamed and jumped up on the couch. The cat came over to the couch, looked up at me as if to say, "Thank you for all the good meals. Here is your gift!" About that time he flung his head back sending the rat flying up in the air. I screamed again. The cat chased the rat and grabbed it. The game started over again; cat flinging the rat in the air, me screaming and the rat being chased down. About twenty long minutes later my husband came rushing in thinking I was being murdered. I was hysterical. The cat had finally killed the rat and was on the floor pawing at it. When my husband finally got the cat and its gift to me out the door, I had

"Tex" Bringing in his Gift.

to tell him the truth. Instead of being angry he laughed, hugged me and became a coconspirator in feeding the cat scraps each evening when he got home from work. Eventually, we came to adopt the cat as our own. We moved to a 'cat friendly home' and named him Tex. He was bow-legged like a cowboy, so what better name?

Tex was a part of our family for eighteen years. He loved to ride in cars, go canoeing and had so many close calls that he proved he fully lived all of his nine lives! To this day I don't know how my landlady and her husband did not hear me screaming and jumping on our couch that fateful night. Oh, and by the way, my husband who did not like cats (he thought) has lived with over twenty during our forty seven years together. Most evenings he falls asleep in his easy chair with one or two cats on his lap, one on the arm of the chair and one on the top of the chair above his head.

You Get the Dog You Need, Not the Dog You Want

Charlene Johnson

As a long-time fan of the famous Cesar Millan, I have made it a point to watch the Dog Whisperer every chance I get. Many seasons ago, I recall Cesar saying: "You get the dog you need, not the dog you want." Well, I thought Cesar missed the mark with that statement, but I'm starting to have second thoughts.

My first dog was Friskey. She was a little terrier mix. She wandered into our neighborhood in Trumbull, Connecticut. Oddly enough, she was lonely and I was lonely. I remember sneaking food out of the house to feed her. After all, what did I know about feeding and caring for a dog? I was only about seven or eight years old and I just wanted to be loved. My folks let me keep Friskey and she became my best friend. She and I would wander in the woods and just get lost together. I was a very happy little girl after adopting Friskey.

Leash laws were not very popular back in the 1950s. Mom and Dad never worried about Friskey roaming the neighborhood. Bad idea. She was eventually hit by a car. I cried, cried and cried some more when I found out that her leg was broken and would never heal properly. It just kind of dangled as she touched it ever so lightly to the ground. For all practical purposes, Friskey was a three-legged dog. But you know what? I loved her even more, because now she was ALWAYS with me. She didn't stray too far from home anymore. But we still found all kinds of interesting things to do around the house. She was my best friend. Even in my loneliest hours, I could count on getting a lick followed by a cold-nosed nudge to cheer me up. Maybe I had it backwards. It's not that she needed me, as much as I needed her. Many a lonely day was filled with sunshine because I had Friskey. I needed her.

But Friskey wasn't my only dog. Years and years later, life experience after life experience including high school, college, having children, and a very rich and fulfilling career—I still managed to have a dog or two here and there. But here I am, staring retirement dead in the eyes when I found Oscar at the Atlanta Humane Society.

Why would I even look for a dog? The children are grown, my career has blossomed and I am very happily busy on a regular basis. My Atlanta home had been burglarized. I was DEVASTATED! Even the best of friends couldn't stay by my side all the time. The internet is a WONDERFUL tool. I searched and searched and searched. Oscar was a beautiful 2-year-old Shar Pei / German Shepherd mix. As an 'older dog' and a fairly uncommon large breed, Oscar was not considered highly-adoptable. True to his Shar Pei personality, Oscar was very aloof and stand-off-ish. True to his German Shepherd personality, Oscar was protective. His bark was outstanding. He always sounded the alert when someone was coming close to the property. Because he was a large working dog, he required training—it was not an option. So off we went to obedience school. Oscar received a certificate for being an outstanding student. He learned all the basic obedience commands and I learned to be firm when dealing with him. Either he was the alpha, or I would be the alpha. Oscar taught me leadership skills. I guess you could say he had just what I needed: companionship, protection and an outstanding example of alpha leadership.

My career required that I travel all across the country and abroad. I was leaving Oscar alone much more than I had expected. I looked for another companion and on the internet found a beautiful Shar Pei mix puppy.

Rachel was only eight weeks old when I picked her out. She had been dropped off in a box at the Cedartown, Georgia Shelter. I fell in love with her big head, brindle markings and wrinkles—lots and lots of wrinkles. I adopted Rachel and immediately changed her name to Shayla. Shayla's job is to calm Oscar and add stability to the pack. As hectic as my work schedule was, Shayla also had a calming effect on me. Did I need it? You bet! Do I still need it? You bet! Had I planned on it working out this way? I never saw it coming! But I am glad that Shay has managed to slow me down a bit.

As luck would have it, Oscar fell in love with my son Randy's Boxer mix: Tookie. You should see Oscar and Tookie. They run together and rough house together. They have never had a spat and both of them seem to just bond together at all times. Randy had no intention of parting with Tookie. So what's a mom to do? I gave Oscar to Randy. Oscar is now living very happily with Tookie. Leaving me with Shayla—who is also a joy. But, I want Shay to be happy too! So back to the internet. Alas, no luck finding another Shar Pei mix.

Now that I have learned 'calm,' I refuse to stress out over a dog. I know what I should do. I'll volunteer to be a

foster mom. Northeast Georgia has a wonderful shelter. I'll check them out for opportunities. The first step is to visit the shelter and see if I am impressed. So far so good. Loud barking—but happy barks.

Wait a minute. There's a dog in that pen. A black dog with little triangle ears. It's a Shar Pei! Can I please walk the Shar Pei? She's wonderful! She's strong. She's confident. She's such a good girl. Ok. I'll foster her. How do you say her name again: Keriah? The paperwork was page after page of info. But I was determined to complete the process. It took me about half-an-hour. Then the quick review session. Then I was told that the application had to be reviewed by the foster committee and my house had to be approved. Oh No! What if Keriah was adopted before I complete the foster home processing? You know what? Never mind. Can I just adopt her?

The rest is history. I adopted Keriah. I admire her for her confidence. The only reservation I have about her is her fits of separation anxiety. She's busted out my screened windows and destroyed my curtains. My door knobs are all scratched up and my window and door trim is gouged. I don't leave Keriah home alone—not inside the house, anyway.

My normal routine when I came home was to excitedly greet my buddies—Shayla and Keriah. With scratches all up and down my arms and legs—just from trying to greet my pack, I needed to change my routine. Now, I walk into my house very calm and controlled. All of my emotions are in check. I breathe in deeply and relax. What a beautiful way to end the work day and start the home-based part of my day. What price would you place on learning this lesson? The price I paid was merely the adoption fee. Keriah is the dog I need to teach me the ultimate relaxation techniques. It's not Pilates or Yoga or Meditation—it's a lovely detox from stress. I have to thank Keriah and Shayla for the lessons—which they reinforce daily. They are my coaches and my companions. I wouldn't trade them for the world!

In closing, Cesar Millan, you are absolutely correct. I get it now. When you take the time to open your heart to a dog, you get the dog you need—you don't just get the dog you want.

Charlene Johnson

If I could give you one thing in life, I would give you the ability to see yourself through my eyes. Only then would you realize how special you are to me. - Unknown

Sailor Boy … Be Careful What You Name Your Pet

Susan S. Dodds

I read once of a young couple who never gave their three children names until they were a few months old and the couple could determine what names seemed to 'fit' them. At the time, I thought this rather odd. However, having named several pets without knowing their sex or their idiosyncrasies and finding out the given name was not fitting . . . maybe that young couple had the right idea after all. I found a kitten once and thinking it was a male, named it George for Curious George, because of its insatiable curiosity. George became Georgi after the first vet visit when it was determined that he was a she.

A little white dog who decided to adopt us by taking up residence on first our porch, then in our home and finally, in our hearts was named Casper (for the ghost). I know, most people would have known the sex difference. Again, after a vet visit, Casper quickly was changed to Cassie.

Probably the most incorrectly named pet of ours, however, was Sailor Boy. My husband is ex-Navy; we lived on a lake; we had a boat and a dock and my children loved the water. When we adopted a little Collie mix from a local shelter, we excitedly decided on the name Sailor. What big plans we had! Sailor was going to boat with us, chase Frisbees off the dock like the other neighborhood dogs and swim in the lake with the children. NOT! Sailor, it turned out was deathly afraid of water. He feared any type of moisture. He refused to go near the lake, whined and shook on his first boat ride. He refused to have anything to do with the game of "chase the Frisbee off the dock and retrieve in the water" that the other neighborhood dogs loved. He shook with fear during each bath and trembled and cried if he got wet from rain. HE HATED WATER! No attempts to calm him around water or to ease him comfortably into a wet situation ever worked. Sailor lived to a ripe old age and we kept his name even though it was an oxymoron.

Happy Rescue Story: Jacki and Lexie (enjoying their car beds on vacation.)

The Life Cycle of a Dog

Dallas Spratt

Newborn puppy
Can't hear
Can't see
Five week old puppy
Mother weans
Learns to play
Four to six months
Independent
Stubborn
Teething and chewing
Adult
All grown up
Loyal and trained
Your "Best Friend"
The life cycle
Begins again

A Pond Story

Emily Lewy

My gardening friends often asked me if I planned to have a "water feature" in my garden. Many times I answered, "I don't think so." It just seemed like a lot work.

But all the talk of water features made me start to think about the happy hours I spent watching goldfish in Mrs. Godwin's pond. When I was a little girl, Mrs. Godwin lived across the street from my grandmother. I loved to visit Grandmother, but one of the main attractions was that pond across the street.

The happy memories of that fishpond so long ago finally made me decide to build one. Wouldn't it be great for my grandchildren to have happy fish memories!

And so, I dived into the project. Dusty Amerson was sixteen years old at the time and he needed spending money. So he agreed to dig the hole. I think it was a lot more work than he expected, but by the end of the day we placed a lining in the hole he had dug.

We laid some nice sized rocks around the edges and added water. The next day, my husband and I bought goldfish. They were little things, maybe an inch or so long. Four were bright gold and the fifth a multi-colored creature of blue, red, gold and white.

We added a filter with a little fountain and several

kinds of water plants. My friend Sarah provided a large pot of cattails that we dug up from her property along the river. And the pond flourished.

I named the multicolored fish, Big Daddy. He was definitely growing faster than the others. The second year, the fish multiplied; and the magic began. Big Daddy had to be the father fish because not a single one of the offspring were solid gold like their mothers.

The most stunning of the half dozen offspring was a beautiful pink fish with deep blue eyes and bright red lips. She looked like a character out of a Disney movie and we named her Hot-lips.

A lot of other wonderful things happened in the pond that year. Bullfrogs moved in. Now these bullfrogs are only about five inches long, but their sounds are truly impressive.

Like when I was a kid, I spent hours watching and admiring that pond. My cat, Abigail, loved it, too. Even my husband likes to tell about the turtle he rescued. The poor thing wandered in and needed help to get out.

We were all so happy enjoying that pond. That is until the day Abigail brought one of the goldfish into the house. She was so proud of that golden gift. But she had to be stopped from going fishing!

My big strong friend, James, arrived to save the day. He and another really strong fellow placed very large rocks all around the pond. Abigail would no longer be able to reach the water, but the rocks gave us an even better perch from which to watch the pond.

Each year the fish and the frogs multiplied. Another pink fish with blue eyes appeared, clearly the daughter of Hot-lips. Each of the different kinds of frogs contributed new sounds, creating beautiful music.

It was all so peaceful. And then, we got another dog. Now the other two dogs were content to sit with Abigail and me beside the pond. But Jocy loves water.

I brought her home from the shelter, gave her a bath, dried her off and let her run in the back yard with the others. She was so happy to be free again. She ran and ran. And then she spied that pond. Before I knew what was happening, she dived in.

I dashed over to help her out because the rocky ledge was too steep for her to get out without help. We were off to the shower for a second bath. Out to run again, and would you believe it that dog dived into the pond again!

After the third bath, she was not allowed back in the yard until I placed tree limbs around the pond. The tree limb barrier worked out great. Jocy now watches the pond like the rest of us without taking a swim.

The old weathered limbs add a quaint, natural look to the scene. Each challenge created by my pets has made the pond more special.

The pond has not proven to be a lot of work. It is an ever-changing project of pure joy. Like the pond from childhood memories, I can spend hours there with family, friends, dogs, cats, fish, frogs, turtles, birds, butterflies, and bugs.

Have you considered adding a water feature to your garden? I highly recommend it.

If your pet could talk, what would it say?
Thank you to the students of
Mrs. Dicken's 2nd Grade.

Don't Let the Cat Out!

Susan S. Dodds

My best friend had a huge cat. I think he may have been half mountain lion.

The cat was named CAT. He was by no stretch of the imagination the biggest, meanest, most fearsome cat I have ever seen. CAT could strike fear in the heart of the bravest cat lover. I am a cat lover! Sometimes I would feed CAT when my friend and her husband were on a trip. A chair was kept by the back door so that when I entered I could fend off CAT with the chair. Many a time I had to keep the chair between the cat and me the entire time I was fixing his tuna. He would pace back and forth snarling and growling at me the entire time I was in the house.

Several years later my friend and her husband listed their house for sale. Since they both worked they allowed real estate agents to show their house when they were at work. They had one request of all agents showing their home. "Don't let the cat out!" Those were the instructions and to make them more emphatic, my friend would tell the real estate agents that the cat was quite large and not at all friendly.

One of the real estate agents, a man named Clyde, had a stuttering problem. It didn't seem to affect his salesmanship. He had a good reputation and my friend was delighted when he called one evening and said he would like to show the house the next day to a prospective buyer. My friend emphasized to Clyde that he was not to let her cat out.

The next afternoon on her way home from work, my friend received a desperate phone call from Clyde. "Mmmrs Jjjjjjjohnson. Ttthis is Clyde. Yyyyour Ccccat got out! Bbbbbut I cccaught him and he is ssssafe inside." My friend thanked Clyde and hurried home. When she opened her door there on her dining room table sat the neighbor's cat, Fritz. He was none too pleased to have been locked up in a strange house. She checked and found her huge monster of a cat hiding under a bed. Anxious to get the neighbor's cat to his own home and explain to her neighbor what must have happened, she scooped him up and hurried down her drive. Another neighbor next door called to her and said, "You missed all of the excitement today." The neighbor went on to say, "Some man was showing your house to a couple of folks. When they left he saw Fritz in your yard and picked him up. Fritz scratched the man to pieces and tore his shirt. I yelled out the window that it was the neighbor's cat. He yelled back, 'I am fffollowing orders.' He threw the cat inside your house and ran to his car and drove away before I could tell him he put it in the wrong neighbor's house."

After that experience the house was shown only when the occupants were home.

Happy Rescue Story: Sickly, nervous, and hungry, this sweet guy began coming to our house for food and attention. We adopted him and now, eight years later, "Carter" is enjoying life!

Cindi Loo Hoo, Shot by the Grinch

Vicki Truelove

Our rescue group received information about a one year old collie that had been declared aggressive and was about to be put to sleep.

Her story started long before she wound up in the shelter. She never received the love and attention she was so deserving of, never had a job, never had a safe place to stay.

So little Cindi Loo Hoo ventured out one day to see what else the world had to offer. Curiosity got the best of her and soon she found herself face to face with the Grinch, his gun and his wicked smile. Try as she might she could not hear his heart beating, nor could she feel the warmth she was seeking. As she stared into his eyes she realized the Grinch's eyes were cold and unfeeling. Without even a blink, she was shot. She felt the stinging pain in her paw and across her chest.

Cindi Loo Hoo ran and ran hoping the pain would stop until she found shelter in a barn. Cindi Loo Hoo had no idea how far she had run but her foot was throbbing. The owners of the barn found her there.

They brought her to the Lumpkin County Animal Shelter saying they could not afford to feed her, that she was a stray. The shelter did an examination and found that Miss Cindi had been shot. Something that the people who turned her in did not mention.

A local vet agreed to do the surgery on her foot. Unfortunately, they had to remove a piece of her foot to successfully remove the bullet.

The shelter director was interested in Cindi and took her home with him to meet his Husky. The Husky didn't care for Cindi's company and went after her, protecting his territory. Scared to death, little Cindi Loo Hoo tried to defend herself, hence, she was now labeled "aggressive".

This little girl, who had been starved for affection and attention, was labeled not adoptable, and therefore, scheduled to die.

When I met her at the shelter, the only thing I saw in her eyes was pure joy that someone had come to see her. Limping slightly still from her surgery, she happily wiggled and turned circles and offered kisses. I walked her down the aisle where others were barking and she paid them no mind. The director brought out another dog, to

test her, and she did not react.

He finally agreed since I was a professional dog trainer, I could rescue Cindi Loo Hoo. Our wonderful volunteer foster, Dawn, picked her up. She was taken for spay surgery before she could be put up for adoption.

The great news is that Cindi Loo Hoo has a forever home. She now lives with a wonderful family in South Florida.

Happy Rescue Story: Sadie, now known as Cindi Loo Hoo, was rescued from a local shelter. Sadie had been shot in the foot and her first toe was removed. When she came to foster she was great with humans but labeled dog aggressive. She was fostered in a home with two other dogs, so it was a rough start, but she soon realized playing with the other dogs was much better than fighting. Sadie was adopted by an adoring couple down in Florida and now has lots of dog friends at the local dog park.

Edith Ann

By Phyllis Ellis

Past the barn and into the woods,
faster, faster she ran.
No time to stop and visit
for she's Edith Ann.
Her bark sounded like
someone screeching in pain,
but really it was just
Edith Ann's way not
to go insane.
She loves to go hunting,
chasing anything that is out there.

A rabbit or a fox.
Oh goodness, Edith Ann
not a bear!
She's a funny looking dog,
part Boston Terrier and maybe Beagle.
She can really look quite silly,
and other times very regal.
She greets you with her
Edith Ann stare,
her lower teeth hang out,
eyes are large and glare.
I still think of her when
Seeing a rabbit hopping away.
It seems like just yesterday
that she was on her way.
Faster and faster she ran,
Oh that was Edith Ann.

My Corgis

Nancy Kondos

It's just the way it is. Draw the Corgi. Pet the Corgi. Color the Corgi. Race with the Corgi. Eat popcorn with the Corgi. Make fun of the Corgi. Whistle for the Corgi. Goo-goo talk with the Corgi. Treasure the Corgi. Brush the Corgi. Brush the Corgi. Brush the Corgi. Stay with the Corgi. Play with the Corgi. Hide from the Corgi. Plump pillows for the Corgi. Kick the ball for the Corgi. Weigh the Corgi. Notice the Corgi. Step over the Corgi. Hoist the Corgi. Make way for the Corgi. Praise the Corgi. Share raspberry crumpets with the Corgi. Stare back at the Corgi. Placate the Corgi. QUACK back at the Corgi. Tickle the Corgi. Jig with the Corgi. Agree with the Corgi. Have story times with the Corgi. Be truthful with the Corgi. Enjoy rainbows with the Corgi. Let the Corgi tiptoe. Let the Corgi chew a shoe or two. Never doubt the Corgi. Never flaunt a cat in front of the Corgi. Be intuitive of the Corgi's wit and wisdom. Fill the Corgi's treat jar forevermore.

Ask The Corgi Queen

Nancy Kondos

The Corgi Queen lives in Buckingham Palace With her Royal Reds throughout which roam Making me wonder if they get into trouble When racing around the sovereign throne.

When the Reds get ornery, does she let them get by And demurely laugh as they get in the trash? Does the Corgi Queen let palatial rubbish pile up

Or does she recycle used socks into Corgi goody troughs? What kind of life does the Queen live With capricious Corgis on the run?

Do her acquaintances think they're really fun? Or do they just pretend,

For to love the Corgi Queen
You must also favor her Reds.

Do they snatch tidbits from pewter plates
And stash salad croutons into secret hiding places While dinner guests stay seated

To hear the Corgi Queen's graces?

Do the Corgis ever lick raspberry sauce Off crowns of queenly custard tops? Do they provide jolly entertainment When thick cream they sip

Paints pasty moustaches
Upon their raven black lips?

Are sugary remnants
Left upon their faces
Soon wiped away
With fine lacy napkins?
What about crumbs
The foraging Reds often drop?
Are there brush-men about
To sweep them right up?
Surely you jest, the Corgi Queen holds nothing against them, Proclaiming they are quite in the right
To show up and fetch whatever delicacy they like.
Does Prince Charles ever cry out, *They're underfoot aplenty!*
Does the Corgi Queen need a preferential license to dare have so many? Does Her Royal Highness ever delay a press conference To give her Reds squeezes?
Does she say God bless you!
When a Corgi impolitely sneezes?

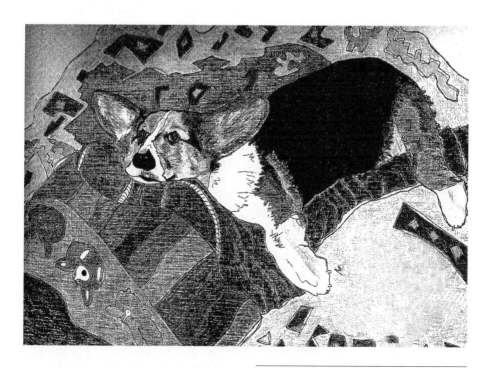

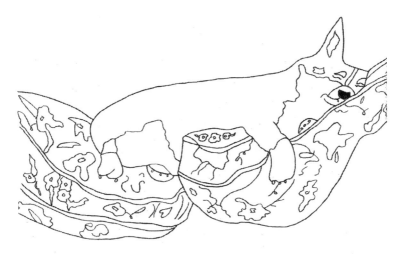

Rest is never frivolous to a prostrate Corgi.

Is the press much too accommodating, Waiting till the Corgis get over their frolicking Before they approach to hear the day's toast? *Corgi Reds Are Never Melancholy!*

Do the Corgis howl as bagpipes play for commemorations?

Do they get under kilts at English dedications? Do they show up tuxedoed for dances majestic

And then round up participants in frenzied fashion?

Do they have treasure trunks filled with stuffed animals to share? Are classic Nyla bones ever put there?

Are the Royal Reds dusted with talcum

From the Queen's favorite scent shop?

Would they rather be recipients of rainbow lollipops?

Does the Corgi Queen have a telly

Where she gathers her Corgis for soccer exhibitions

And tea carts filled with biscuits of cinnamon?

Please tell me if they have any habits upon which the Corgi Queen frowns. Or at night does she recount the Corgis' capers as stupendous When she sees them in the Royal Nursery all bedded down?

Why Shouldn't Our Corgi Have A Shoe?

Nancy Kondos

Why shouldn't our Corgi have a shoe? He likes to inherit them.

They're so delicious to chew.

He especially likes to have fun

And pull out the tongue,

Gnarl the shoestrings, drool down the sides, Nibble at the toe then nap with his muzzle inside Where the well of the heel is set low to his liking.

So why shouldn't our Corgi have a shoe? Give him two

And a third for when he chews the others thin.

When it's his birthday

I'll smile at him and say,

Remember the shoes?

Not one, not even two, but three. Now go play!

Writing Morning Pages
Nancy Kondos

Good morning dear morning pages.

It's Monday morning, almost eight thirty a.m.

My hair is already ball-cap flat.

Wrestling with the house's chill, I button on my blue-checked flannel shirt.

There are my cherished colored pencils. Let's soon get them in hand.

Squiggle lines to suit a Corgi face

Defined by dreams of delinquent dew

That whet his delight to slip and slide in one quick motion, Sailing as if on top of the ocean,

And landing ahoy with his snout thrust out,

Glistening with the memory of the fading morning mist.

It's times like this that Corgi charms persist to rule my imagination

With calibrating notions that the Pembroke is worth all charted devotion.

For both Mr. Byron and South-8 have instigated my ceaseless wonder

At bold chests rolling out thunder under ears attuned for strict mischief

Guided by spry Napoleonic legs superbly suited for circular navigation.

Stream Check

Nancy Kondos

On a stream check with South-8. Startling to have him
    rush past
Then stop dead ahead to glance back Making sure I'm
    still there
Treading on sun-cracked ground
Or cushioned clover.
Water in the stream pristine. South-8 gets in.
Bites it.
Turns his ear into a sieve
Funneling nature's cold water While mud clings to his
    underside.
We travel further.
South-8 jumps over tree-dropped branches.
We turn toward home. An uphill chore.
South-8 adopts a stick. We arrive on the
    porch.
Gate closes.
I refresh
    South-8's wa-
    ter bowl. Take
    off my dirty
    shoes.
An exuberant start for
    the day.
Now it's time to
    write dear Cor-
    giisms

Corgi Hair

Nancy Kondos

South-8 sheds gallons of hair
That flows under beds and soon disappears 'Til guests
    arrive and it scatters about
Making them all wonder did the vacuum break down.
The mice collect it for their minuscule homes.
It cradles their babies in plenty of puff.
Then promotes hardy allergies in noses that are stuffed.
Our Corgi's double coat is full of it.
Just poke your finger in to get through to the skin.
Makes a sudden indentation that quickly smooths over
    thick.
There's good reason for such lustrous protection As mud
    and gook can be found during rainy days On most
    country roads and outdoorsy play places.
I don't mean to scare you, but Corgi lovers beware For
    once a Corgi Tri makes his way onto your bed He'll
    claim your pillow to rest his noble head Leaving tan,
    white and black hairs all at once
To fly into your nose when later you kerplunk Onto your
    pillowcase for a good night's sleep
And instead spend the night ah-chooing at your feet.
South-8 insists on scampering about
Shaking from nose to curt tail in the house Furiously

spraying a thousand hairs into the air.

We often count them as they cling to our britches Whenever we sit on the living room couch.

Whatever shall we do to make South-8 stop? He that sheds in all our home spaces.

He that rules with rude QUACKING triumphs. He that rules with stubborn inclination. He that rules with four paws that easily drop Into a typical squatty Corgi plop.

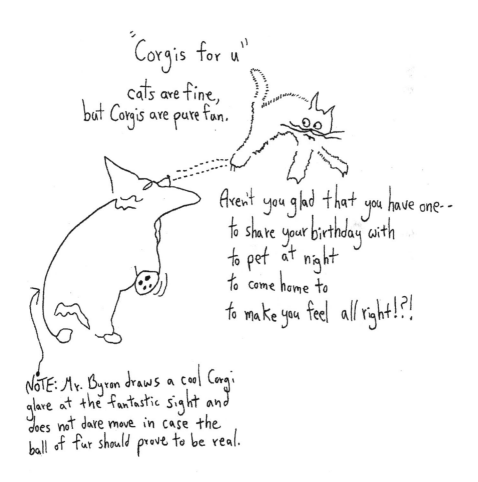

Small or Tall?

Nancy Kondos

Yay!

I'm an Artist of Little Things That Matter With a degree in Corgiism

Letting me ridiculously debate

Whether a Corgi is a little thing like small Or a big thing like tall.

Indeed South-8 is pound-size impressive. Yet Tall?

Don't think so.

I've never known him

To meet height requirements

For carnival rides at the county fair.

How silly to even think

Unless one is forever linked to Corgiism.

But there once was a Corgi who dared

To suddenly appear in the mirrored fun house

Only to be scared of his eerie ears following him about.

Way up high they soared above his snout Reducing him to a shy countenance Ruining his reputation as a gadabout.

So there he squatted in anticipation, Looking at his head in extreme agitation.

Moral: A Corgi should no doubt be careful when running about

As he may be chastened by erratic ears in a packed fun house.

A Corgi can be tall

if he stands upon a rock.

Observation of a Corgi's Interest in Self

Nancy Kondos

You'll know an uppity Corgi when you meet one For his nose is held much higher

Than the crown of a grand mushroom.

That's very high indeed.

Don't compliment him about his remarkable tip-top, no-flop ears Just because he has them.

That will promote a chest full of vanity.

Wait 'til his ears go into full gear

And swallow sounds down his hearing canals Then reward him with a to-the-point comment.

My how your teepee ears funnel every sort of a peep

I was quite impressed as you must have guessed

By their twitching manner and your bobbing head that followed about.

Just imagine South-8 catching the sound-waves of a summer's eve toad Leaping over a double-stemmed mushroom at the height of its crown And landing on his squishy feet.

Kersplat is maybe the sound for that. But only South-8 really knows.

Mr. Byron

Nancy Kondos

Mr. Byron was a Tri-Color Pembroke Welsh Corgi Whom
    I adopted with my first husband
From an Arlington, VA, animal shelter.
Mr. Byron went with me wherever I homesteaded. From
    a neighborhood house with a yard to boast
To a rented condo where leashed walks were a necessity
    And my divorce would become final.
And finally the bought condo
Where he'd argue with neighbor dog Patches
Every time he climbed the stairs past
Patches' second story turf.
That's where I began to rebuild my single life.
Mr. Byron slept on top of couch cushions Designed with-
    out a Corgi in mind
Yet beneficial to his art of meditation
Where he escaped in slumber upon floral fibers That ha-
    bitually sank to his shape.
Mr. Byron preferred cool ceramics of the bathroom in-
    terior, Squeezing in toilet side or bathtub wide
Where outside nois-
es were less likely to
intrude In his ven-
ue with a window
only two by two Slid
shut to favor a re-
luctance to fill his
ears With piercing
residue like squeals
of mockingbirds

Who only yesterday flew tempestuously
On cue at the Corgis unprotected head
Riveted toward their protected maple tree nest.
I always caught the doorknob in my belly
As I squeezed in and out of the privy
While the Corgi sought privacy in porcelain pure white.
Cool.
Huggable.
Other rooms did not quite suffice For much of his bid-
ing time. When much younger though The world
was his welcoming map,
Including stair steps that were cleared in stride
By four paws gliding high in unison.
SOLD I was
The first time I laid eyes on him.
Great white chest.
Wearing a mask of red
Over a black face.
Divided by a white stripe running from brow to snout.
Mr. Byron took over the mail slot in the front door
And shredded paper items when they were still air-
borne. He was highly spirited in his inherited
short stature And liked to smush his nose in blan-
ket folds.
Often chased ankles and toes.
He added great zest because he was so bold.
My new husband and I faced Mr. Byron's
Slowing-down days together
By carrying his arthritic body up and down unconquerable
stairs.
We would ease him to the sidewalk curb
Where he could peer toward the nearby park
And dream of former days when he easily roamed.

Sophie

Nancy Garrison

Hi everyone!

My name is Sophie and I am a small Cocker Spaniel. I was rescued from an animal shelter by a very nice lady who just KNEW I would love kids! It turned out that she knows my new mommy and took me to meet her. It was love at first sight! I love my new family so much. They have lots of company all the time, so I get to see new people and sometimes even kids! My mommy walks me every day and gives me treats when I am good (which is most of the time). She could tell right away that I might be a good reader so she enrolled me in the READ program. I practice all the time with the kids that stop by our house. I have a job now that is LOTS of fun! I visit nursing homes and the school for the Head Start Program. My mommy reads a book to all the children in the class and I get to sit beside her right in the middle of all the kids. It is great! They keep calling me a Therapy dog, but I don't know what that means. All I know is that I make lots of people smile, and that's what I really want to do. I am getting better at reading, but sometimes I need help. Will you please read to me at the Lumpkin County Library? We are there on the first Saturday of every month, as long as the Library is open. You can also e-mail me if your parents say it's ok. Sophie_G@ READingPaws.org

Your next best friend!
Sophie

Tex, the Travelin' Cat
Susan S. Dodds

Our cat, Tex, was quite an adventurous traveler. You almost had to see it to believe it. He was part of our family for eighteen years and during that time he lived in four states and traveled (with our family) throughout the West, Midwest, South, New England and Canada. He loved to ride in cars!

In the spring of 1968, my husband and I took a trip from Michigan to Florida. Of course Tex had to go with us—no kennel for him! My husband built a little cage for Tex so he could ride comfortably and safely in the back of our little red Studebaker convertible with the top down. He loved to have the wind in his face and to feel his whiskers blow. We had not gone very many miles when I turned to check on Tex in his cage on the back seat. Much to my shock, Tex was not in the cage. The wily little guy had somehow opened the cage door and was fast asleep on the seat with a contented smile on his face. After two more futile attempts to keep him 'safe' in his cage, we decided to let him have his way. Tex thoroughly enjoyed his ride on the back seat to and from FL with the convertible top down all the way.

Though he was not fond of being wet, Tex loved to go canoeing with us. He would stand at the front of the canoe as if directing us through the water. Once when we got too close to shore, he jumped from the canoe onto the bank and disappeared into the woods. We waited about an hour, calling and coaxing him to come back to the canoe. Dejected and fearing the worst, we were debating what to do next, when he appeared from behind a tree.

He walked over to the canoe, jumped in and looked at us as if to say, "OK, hurry up. I've done my exploring, now let's go!"

Tex's love of travel did get him into trouble at times. Friends and relatives learned quickly that when they came to visit us, they dared not leave their car windows down. Tex, happy vagabond that he was, would jump in, ride home with the visitors and we would receive a call from them saying, "Tex is visiting. Come and get him."

Once, Tex disappeared for over two weeks. We looked everywhere and finally had to sadly resign ourselves to the fact that he was not coming home. Wrong! Tex appeared at our door in the middle of a storm, tired and hungry. His loud wailing signaled us that he was home. After he had been thoroughly dried, hugged and had eaten heartily, he fell asleep on his favorite bed. We could only surmise that Tex had gotten into a delivery or mail truck and ridden the route with the driver. Somehow, he had found his way home from wherever he had landed. I seemed to notice a certain glint in his eyes when we would wonder aloud where he had been for over two weeks. If only he could have talked!

"TEX" in the Wind

If your pet could talk, what would it say?
Thank you to the students of Mrs. Dicken's 2nd Grade.

Charlie and Little Bit
By Phyllis Ellis

"One more time being put into this box and I'll yeow! I do hope it's not to the veterinarian. I hate those shots. Other times in this box have taken me on long journeys."

"Oh, hush-up, Little Bit, and give me more room in this box! More rooooooooom!" yelled Charlie.

Charlie, a yellow tabby cat has lived in numerous apartments in New York, Atlanta and now in the country, along with Little Bit, a black and white cat. They grew up together and have learned to adapt to different living situations.

"Where do you suppose we're going?" asked Little Bit.

"Hey, I don't have a clue," answered Charlie. "No one ever tells me anything. I heard something about moving to a farm."

"What's a farm?" asked Little Bit.

"Well," said Charlie as he peeped through the small opening in the box, "I lived on a farm when I was a small kitten. In fact, if you must know . . . I was born in a barn."

"I sort of remember you telling me that when we first met." said Little Bit as she started washing her paw. "We sure have moved around a lot."

"Wow . . . easy does it, easy does it. Don't rock us too much!" Charlie yowled as the box was then picked up and placed into the VW Van.

They reached the farm in about an hour. That can be a long time for a couple of cats in a cat carrier. Forrest and Phyllis, who decided to move to the country, brought along their two cats and a large Shepherd type dog with a long tail and a lop-sided ear, named Banjo.

The moving van right behind the VW bus proceeded to pull into the driveway of a very old, dilapidated farmhouse. Charlie and Little Bit looked through the peep holes of the box to see a large barn and a smaller barn to the right of the old house.

"Meow . . . are we going to live here?" asked Little Bit.

Charlie looked closer at the barns, the old out-buildings, and looked through another hole to see lots of trees and pastureland. It sure wasn't the city anymore, he thought to himself.

"I sure hope so. We can do a lot of exploring around here."

"I love it! I love it!" barked Banjo.

He'd been here before when Phyllis and Forrest looked at the place and had decided to buy the twenty acre farm.

As the moving folks moved furniture into the house, the two cats were kept in a small bathroom, along with the kitty litter box, food and water. Banjo would run in and out, jumping around with excitement of all that was going on.

"We're here, we're here!" Banjo kept barking. "I can't believe I'm going to live here!"

The movers left and it became quiet as Phyllis and Forrest sat down and looked around. The house would need a lot or repair work.

"What have we done?" Phyllis asked, as she looked around at all the garbage that was left, broken windows, ugly wallpaper and dents in some of the walls.

"It'll be okay." Forrest answered. "We can get this place in shape."

Phyllis let the two cats out of the bathroom.

"Well, it's about time," said Little Bit as she started looking around. "That bathroom was terrible."

"Hey, look at this place!" Charlie exclaimed, as he too started to wander around the house. They both sniffed the furniture and boxes left here and there.

"Guess this is our new home," Charlie said as he looked in each room.

Banjo was still excited as he lay by the sofa and panted with joy. He loved the place. Charlie and Little Bit were a little overwhelmed by all the different rooms. As long as they knew where the kitty litter was and where they were going to be fed, everything was okay with them.

That evening, the cats slept on the bed and Banjo slept next to the bed to be close to their human friends.

After a few days of getting acclimated to the house,

Charlie and Little Bit were able to go outside and explore.

"Look, Charlie . . . look at all the places to explore!" Little Bit said as she investigated what used to be a smokehouse. The old wooden door had a hole at the bottom, just enough room for a cat or some small animal to go through. She glanced around to see boxes and tools and lots of little cubby holes.

"I can smell mice in this place." Charlie said, as he too wandered around the small wooden building. "Oh, yeah, this place has lots of potential for hunting mice."

When they reached the large barn, it was huge to them. It had four large stalls and a tack room. The second floor was empty, except for some leftover junk. It had a place to throw down hay into the stall's hayracks. The area could probably store two hundred bales of hay, maybe more. There was another small landing above that floor which used to store grain. The barn was old and rundown, but still very useable.

"Who are you?" growled a calico cat. "What are you doing here?" She hissed and arched her back at Charlie and Little Bit.

"We just moved here . . . don't get all upset with us . . . who are you and what are you doing here?" questioned Charlie. He stood his ground and wagged his tail as a warning. The cats stared at each other as they dared to see who would make the first move.

"That's enough!" Little Bit said. "I'm going back to the house." She ran off and Charlie did not take his eyes off the stray cat. The calico cat slowly backed off and went under the floorboards to tend to her family. She had five kittens that were only a couple of weeks old. Charlie watched and then walked away. "It's okay, we won't bother you." Charlie said as he started back towards the house.

"You might want to make an appearance to our humans, who are the new owners of this place. You might get a meal or two, especially if you show them your kittens."

"Thanks." the calico answered. "I'm getting tired of hunting for mice and trying to watch these kittens, too. What about the dog?"

"Banjo?" Charlie replied, as he watched Banjo sniffing around the barn.

"He's a pushover. Just let him know he shouldn't mess with you and you'll be fine."

Just then, a chicken walked by, clucking as she passed the cats. "Cluck, cluck, where should I put this egg I'm going to have? Cluck, cluck."

Charlie had never seen a bird that size. "Who's that?" he asked.

"Oh, that's Miss Hen." replied the calico cat. "She was left behind when they gathered up the chickens and took them away. She's no threat to us. Well, I've got to tend to my kittens."

Charlie went back to the house. Little Bit was waiting for him and asked what he had talked about with that "stray." The back door opened. It was suppertime! They came inside and as they were eating, Charlie began thinking about the calico cat and her kittens.

The next day, Phyllis and Forrest inspected the different barns and outbuildings with excitement. As they came to the big barn, Phyllis could hear the kittens mewing.

"I hear some kittens." She said to Forrest. "I think they're under the floor of the tack room. Here, kitty, kitty." She knelt down to look between the boards. The calico cat came out and presented her kittens, one by one.

"Look, oh look how cute they are!" Phyllis exclaimed. "I need to get them some food and water. The last owners must have just left them here." She ran to the house and within a few minutes came back with bowls of cat food and water. It didn't take the cat family long to realize they were getting a meal.

They wouldn't leave the barn area, so each day Phyllis would bring food and water out to them.

Miss Hen was also getting a meal of scratch food and water as Forrest discovered her that same day.

After a few days of exploring the buildings on the farm, Charlie and Little Bit decided to explore the field and woods. This was a great adventure to them, since they had lived most of their lives in apartments in the city or suburbs.

"Come on, hurry, we've got lots to see!" Charlie yelled.

"Okay, okay . . . but where are we going?" replied Little Bit.

"I don't know, let's just run into the woods and see what there is to see."

The woods were full of tall hardwood and pine trees, birds flying around and squirrels running from branch to branch, a small creek flowing across the rocks to form a small waterfall. The two cats wandered through the brush and even drank water from the creek. Eating grass was a treat, even if it did make them throw up.

They saw a snake, but decided to leave it alone. They were so interested in all that was around them, they wandered for hours and hours. Before they knew it, the sun had gone down. It was dark and they had never really been out at night. They were always inside a house before it became dark.

"Now what?" Little Bit asked. "I have no idea where we are or how to get back. Do you?"

"Well, I think it's back that way . . . or maybe it's this way." Charlie turned around and looked in different directions. He, too, was lost. "Cats don't get lost!" he said. "It must be this way."

The moon was out and strange shadows fell on the ground. Different night-time noises were heard such as owls, crickets, and other sounds that they were not familiar with.

They started running through the woods, hoping to find the way home, when all of a sudden Little Bit yelled out, "Ooooooowwwwwww! I'm hurt! Charlie, I'm hurt!"

Charlie stopped and ran back to her to see her stomach and back leg were caught in a barbed wire fence. She was bleeding and he could tell she was in great distress.

"I can't seem to help you. I don't know what to do." Charlie cried.

"Go back home, Charlie." Little Bit cried. "I don't think I can make it."

Charlie went on, hoping that maybe she could get loose and catch up with him. He wasn't sure where he was or where home was. He kept thinking about Little Bit, but now he wasn't even sure how to find her. He just wanted to get home.

It was a week before he found his way back to the farmhouse. It was raining and late at night, but he recognized the house. He meowed outside the porch door.

"Hey, anyone home?" Charlie cried. "Helloooo, I'm back!"

Sure enough, the door opened and Phyllis and Forrest were glad to see him. They dried him off and fed him, and he curled up on their bed and slept like he had never slept before. He was glad to be home again.

Meanwhile, Little Bit was weak from losing so much blood. She tried and tried to get loose from the wire. She shivered as the rain came down on her. She was frightened and wished she had never listened to Charlie. "I'll never go anywhere with you again, Charlie. I'm so angry with you I could spit!"

Finally, she just gave it a yank and tore away from the barbed wire. Her skin inside her back leg was cut badly, but she was loose. Again, she started bleeding, but she kept licking it and finally the bleeding stopped. She would now just rest for a while.

The next morning, she began to slowly walk through the woods. She was able to make her way to the creek to drink water. She even caught a mouse, which she had never done before. She was hungry and weak from the injury.

She was alone in a place she didn't know. "I just want to be home again." she cried.

One morning, she came across an area that looked familiar to her. Yes, it was the pasture behind the house. She could see the barns and the farmhouse. "Yes, yes, I'm here! I'm home! I've found my way home! Charlie, Charlie, I'm home!"

Phyllis opened the door and there was Little Bit, skinny, injured, but home at last. "She's back! Little Bit is back!" Phyllis cried out.

Little Bit was still hurting from the severe cut, but she was glad to be home and was also very, very hungry and tired.

That same day, Phyllis took her to the veterinarian to have her checked out. He gave her a shot of penicillin and some cream to put on the wound.

Little Bit was home and for a long time wouldn't step outside of the house. She also didn't want anything to do with Charlie and his big ideas about exploring.

Charlie stayed close to home, too. He did like hunting for mice, and would sit in the backyard, very still, until a mouse or shrew would come by and then he'd catch it. He was pretty good at that. Charlie enjoyed the country life. Little Bit, on the other hand, was content to be inside most of the time. If she did go out, it was only in the yard or barn.

The two cats shared long lives together. They did have to put up with other cats and dogs that came into their lives as they lived the country life. But they were the senior cats and were respected by the younger additions to the household.

Sweet Doc

Susan S. Dodds

Having had many pets over the years, I have reached a conclusion. Each dear pet was sent to teach me a lesson about unconditional love and the abundance of spiritual knowledge that one can learn and experience from having a pet in one's home.

Over the years I have rarely planned an adoption or sought out a new pet family member. They just seem to 'happen' to find me.

"Doc" was one of those special teachers who taught a lesson our family will never forget.

I am a morning person. I taught school for thirty plus years and made it a habit to arrive at the high school where I taught before any other faculty or staff (except Bobby, the custodian). I arrived early so that I could grade papers and plan my day. Bobby and I would have morning chats and then I would go to my classroom to work. One morning as I was walking from the parking lot to the school, I saw a very skinny tiger cat standing by the school's front door. I stooped down to pet him and could feel nothing but bone and ribs. I reached into my lunch bag, pulled out my peanut butter sandwich and offered him a small bite. He gobbled it and actually began purring. Halfway through the cat's breakfast, Bobby, the

custodian opened the door. "That cat got into the office last night and s*&# all over. I cleaned it up, but if the principal finds out, he will have a fit!" Finished with his sandwich, the cat wandered away and I went to my classroom to work.

Later that morning, during my planning period, I was called to the office by the school secretary. The P.A. in my room clicked and the message was loud and clear, "Mrs. Dodds, YOUR cat got into the office again. Mr. Jones (the principal) will call animal control and the cat will go to the shelter unless you come and get him." What was I to do? MY CAT? That Bobby!

The secretary had deposited the cat in a large store room off the main office. When I peeked in, he was fast asleep on a pile of rags. I told her to give me 'til the end of the day to decide what to do with him. She told me she would, but that she just hoped the principal did not hear the cat or happen into the storage room.

At the end of the day I retrieved 'my cat' and began my thirty mile drive home. I called my husband to warn him that I was bringing home another uninvited guest. He told me to make a stop at the local vet's office and have the cat examined and given his shots. I agreed because we had four other cats at home and I did not want them exposed to some unknown disease.

After examining the cat, Dr. Potter, the vet, told me that he figured his age at somewhere between sixteen to eighteen years of age! He also told me that the cat would need an operation immediately for a thyroid condition. I explained the situation and told him that I was just 'fostering the cat.' I told him that I felt sure I could find someone in the school system to give him a home and that I planned to start networking the next day. I was extremely upset because I had just paid $200 for shots and an examination. I did not have the finances to pay for the impending operation that was needed. Dr. Potter excused himself and left the room. He came back shortly with a big smile on his face. He told me that one of their new vets had never done this type of operation. She would do it pro bono for the experience of doing it. I thanked him profusely.

For the next three weeks, I emailed, called and networked furiously to find a home for the little guy. I had three responses. All three wanted to make him as an outside cat. I just did not feel good about that. My cats are indoor cats and I felt at this cat's age, he needed to be inside. After three and a half weeks of daily visitations to the cat at the vet's and no luck with finding him a home, I decided that he was going to have to come home with me.

Dreading the huge boarding bill I was going to owe, I left school one day determined to pay the bill and take him home to meet my other four cats. I was shocked and so grateful when the receptionist at the vet's office said, "Dr says, 'no charge'." I thanked her profusely and will be eternally grateful for the kindness of that doctor and his clinic. While the cat was staying at the vet's, I had named him "Doc". I felt that was fitting since a "Doc" had been so kind and had saved his life.

Doc put on weight. He never got a lot of meat on his bones, but he began to look healthier. He had a very loud cry. He also had a habit of staring intently at people and objects. He loved riding in our car. He would sit on my lap and put his front feet on the dashboard. Since he had obviously been an outside cat, he would occasionally sit at the door and howl. We would attach a leash to his little collar and walk him around the yard. He seemed to enjoy the walks. They seemed to sate his appetite for the outdoors. The strangest behavior Doc exhibited, however, was with our two year old grandson. When Ethan came to visit, replete with his typical two year old noise, flailing arms, tiny running feet and full of energy, the other cats hid. Not Doc! He loved Ethan. He would purr, sit in Ethan's lap and follow him around. If Ethan took a nap, Doc was right there on the bed with him. He always wanted to touch Ethan. In fact, often times Doc's paw and Ethan's hand would be touching. They were best buddies.

Two and a half months after Doc came to be a part of our family, I was vacuuming one day. All of the cats disappeared as usual, frightened by the loud noise. All disappeared . . . except for Doc. He did not move an inch from his bed on one of the recliners. When I glanced over and saw that he was not responding, I turned off the machine and went over to the chair. I snapped my fingers, clapped my hands and shouted. Doc did not budge nor did he awaken. I touched him lightly and he jolted awake with a loud 'Meowwww.'

Suddenly everything became very clear and I felt so silly for not having noticed before. Doc was stone deaf! How that little old guy had survived outside for who knows how long is a wonder. Thank goodness I had not let him go to one of the people who had offered to adopt him as an outside cat!

No wonder his cry was so loud! No wonder loud noises did not frighten him! This explained why he was not afraid in the car.

Within a week, Doc and I had worked out some sign language between us. He was a quick student. He actually learned the come, stop, head-shaking for no signs.

His deafness and his ability to rise above it made him all the more special to us. At Christmas we took Doc in the car to see Christmas lights. He purred and purred and turned his little head from side to side to take in all the lights.

Doc graced our lives for a little over a year. When his little, old body gave out, we were so sad and missed him so much. But through our tears, we had to smile, also. What love and what an abundance of understanding he gave us. And, I would like to think that we helped make sweet Doc's last year a happy one.

My Path of Loved Ones

Cecile Thompson

In August of 2008 I lost my dog George to heart failure. Seven years before, I rescued George after his owners decided they no longer wanted him and asked that he be put to sleep. How could they toss aside such a loving dog? He was so affectionate, his fur soft as silk. Charlie, our darling cock-a-poo, was fifteen when I brought George home. They spent three fun-filled years together before God took Charlie home at the age of eighteen.

When George was diagnosed with a failing heart, the doctors gave him six to nine months to live. George's heart was so full of love, though, that he stayed with us two more years. I had always prayed that I would be with him when God took George home. One day, as he ran down the stairs to greet me, he had a fatal heart attack. There's a big red heart painted on my basement floor where he laid before going to heaven. My other rescue dog Grace and I mourned the loss of George but it soon came time to search for another homeless brother or sister—our house was just too empty and silent.

Weeks went by, and so many times I left the adoption shelter empty-handed and discouraged because I just couldn't find the "right" dog. One Sunday I went in the small dog/puppy area, looking in the cages and saddened by all the homeless dogs staring at me in hopes I'd open their cage and bring them home. I tried, but couldn't bring myself to look any longer and left. For some reason, though, I went back in the shelter, to where the big dogs are held. Why was I being drawn there? I walked aimlessly through the aisles, trying not to make eye contact. Then, out of the corner of my eye, I saw this tiny dog lying on a cot. He was so small I almost missed seeing him. I said, "what are you doing in here with these big dogs?" as if expecting an answer. He timidly came towards me, head down and tail slightly wagging. He was so skinny that his hip and rib bones stuck out, looking like his skin barely draped over them. His little face was sunken in and he looked so forlorn. I stuck my fingers through the gate holes and he licked them sheepishly.

Then came an announcement that the shelter was closing. I left quickly, without looking at him again because I was crying and I didn't want to see the disappointment in his dejected face. I felt guilty because I still missed George. I stopped by the desk to inquire about the little dog, but the woman said she didn't have any information on him, other than he was seized by animal control. On the way home, I couldn't get the picture of this sweet abandoned dog from my mind, wondering what his past must hold.

That night Grace met me at the door when I came home. I detected a look in her eye of disappointment that I didn't have a companion for her. Both our hearts were empty and broken, still missing George. While we took our walk, I decided to return to the shelter the next day for another visit with the skinny little cocker spaniel. I decided I would adopt him and call him Eddie, after my late brother. I wasn't sure how my mom would feel about this, though. She didn't think I was ready for another dog, not to mention naming one after Ed.

I arrived at the shelter when it opened, walked past the desk and entered the large dog area, heading straight to the cage to get Eddie. He was gone! My heart was broken, and I began to cry. Where could be have gone? I ran to the front desk and was told he had been moved to another cage. I think he sensed I came back for him because I could hear the beating of his tail against the cage even before I turned the corner. He saw me, but this time didn't hesitate to greet me and lick my hand again. I opened the door and picked him up. I could feel his ribs in my hands and when his eyes met mine, they were so sunken, but saying, "please take me home". He clung to me as if for his life. What a beautiful face lick, lick, lick!

I was leery about bringing him outside to meet my mother, unsure of her reaction. She was waiting in the car. It was Monday, September 19 and her eighty-seventh birthday. She didn't move very well, but when I walked towards her with this little bundle of joy, she got out of the car, held out her arms, and said, "Come to Grandma!" What better birthday gift could there be? Since the shelter could only guess that he was a year old, we made Eddie's birthday the same as Mom's and we took him to the get acquainted room. Eddie was so playful, retrieving the ball and jumping in our laps. I adopted him and took him home. When he entered the door, Gracie was standoffish for a moment. They sniffed each other and began to play. Eddie was very, very fast, loved to bring the tennis ball back, and never seemed to get tired. He jumped in bed and from one couch to another. Our home was happy again.

Six weeks later everything changed.

As he began to put on weight, Eddie's ability to walk had declined dramatically, as well as his energy level. Grace attempted to play with him, but Eddie could barely walk. After numerous trips to our local veterinarian and the University of Georgia, the doctors were unable to diagnose his illness. They prescribed medicine and Eddie's condition slowly began to improve. He became more alert and happy. He resumed playing with Grace, but still had difficulty walking. He was the most comfortable sitting up so I found a baby carriage to put him in when Grace and I took our walks. People strolled by expecting to see a cute baby. Imagine their surprise when they saw Eddie! Everyone said he was the sweetest dog they'd ever seen. I beamed like a proud mother!

Soon after, though, Eddie's condition got worse again. I carried him most of the time, and he rarely felt like getting out of his carriage during our walks. He slept a lot and didn't play much with Grace. He wanted to, I could tell, but after a few tugs on the toy, he dropped it and lay down. He looked so sad and disappointed. When I came home, he would wag his tail so hard back that he'd fall over. He didn't know he was ill, but I did.

I desperately tried to find out exactly what was wrong with Eddie but without success. The vets couldn't figure it out either and my mind became cloudy with all the confusion. Medical terms I didn't understand and doctors trying to find an answer to what was plaguing Eddie. Was it spinal? Birth defect? Abuse from his former owner? Cancer? Inherited? Euthanasia was also mentioned, but that was NOT an option to me. Eddie was tired but happy and not in pain, so I decided to take care of him no matter what. His MRI didn't show anything, nor did a biopsy. I pleaded for help from organizations, canine handicap websites, and pet resources in hopes that someone would know of a similar situation, and provide advice, but the answer never came.

After realizing that Eddie would probably never be physically normal, I decided to accept him being lame, and make the best of it. I found a vest that wrapped around his little body with a handle to carry him in and we went to the lake every day for months to swim. At first he was in a life jacket until he was strong enough to swim by himself and soon his legs were getting stronger. He seemed so happy and he loved all the attention he was getting from everyone. I accepted the fact that Eddie would always be impaired but knew that the three of us could have a happy life together. Eddie just needed extra attention and, of course, Gracie got her share too.

Soon after, though, I saw blood on the pillow where Eddie slept. I took him to the vet for what he thought was an abscessed tooth. The doctor opened Eddie's mouth said, "Oh my gosh." When I looked in Eddie's mouth I screamed in horror and fell on the floor. He had a tumor inside the top of his mouth that no one had seen before. I was in shock. How could my happy dog have this growing inside him? Again, we took the long, heart-wrenching drive back to UGA where everyone was also stunned. There was nothing anyone could do for him now. The news was devastating and the drive home silent except for me crying. After all we'd been through in our short year together, this news was surreal; and I didn't want to think about our next step. Eddie's health quickly deteriorated. Just a year ago my mother and I celebrated both her and Eddie's birthday. This year we tried to enjoy the day with party hats and ice cream but frowns and sadness were on our faces instead of smiles.

Two days later I took Grace and Eddie back to UGA. We all sat on the floor as the doctor gave Eddie the shot that would make him go to sleep forever. He was so peaceful. Grace licked his face and said goodbye. Then she licked the tears from mine. It was so hard for me to do, but I knew it was best for Eddie. I didn't want him to suffer. The ride home was worse than the last.

That was two years ago. My mom passed away recently, just before her birthday. She would have been ninety next week, and Eddie would have been four. I miss them terribly, but know they've crossed the RAINBOW BRIDGE and are happy and healthy again. No walking cane for mom and no stroller for Eddie. Grace and I will celebrate their birthdays and remember all the wonderfully happy times we shared with them.

We never know on what path God will lead us and suffering the pain of losing a loved one is unbearable. But not having them with you along the road of life, sharing wonderful memories and laughs, would be far worse.

Gracie and I now share our home with Noodles, a rescued little cock-a-poo, two cats, and three birds!

HAVE FUN IN HEAVEN MOM,
CHARLIE, GEORGE, AND EDDIE

Lady's Story

Carolyn Upton

We first met Lady at TLC sometime during 2000. She was three years old, and we found a nice family to adopt her.

She was the perfect pet for them. She stayed in the yard, walked without a leash, and many times pulled their toddlers back from the road. She stayed in her loving home until the spring of 2011. We had some really fierce electrical storms, and lightning struck the corner of their garage. Both Lady and their cat ran away.

We don't know how Lady managed to survive for more than six months on her own. The cat is still not accounted for. There were probably some good Samaritans who fed her. That is very common in our rural community. Many times people move to another place and leave the strays that "came up" on them years before. After all, it wasn't their dog! Eventually someone called animal control to pick her up, and on October 10 she was brought into the Lumpkin County Animal Services (LCAS) facility.

The first step that they probably do is to scan the dog for a microchip. Lady didn't have one, because TLC wasn't providing them with the adoption 11 years ago as they do now. They noticed the rabies tag from 2008 and called the vet. The family moved three years ago and changed vets, so their contact information was not current. Lady was placed in an outside run, and was deemed unadoptable because of her age and the fact that adult black dogs rarely get adopted. Her picture was not taken, and she was not advertised on Petfinder. She was not listed as a found dog on the shelter's lost and found web site. She was doomed.

But then, something miraculous happened! TLC participated in the Gold Rush festival in Dahlonega, and over 100,000 people came from far and wide to enjoy the beautiful mountains and the perfect fall weather. Our booth was one of the best attended at the festival, and 20 dogs and cats found their forever families! Our little pair of dachshunds went to a wonderful couple from Palm Beach, Florida, and our Joy, rescued from starvation by a local resident, went to a loving home with the vendor across from our booth! People come from near and far for this festival, and many of them stopped to love on our sweet dogs, cats, kittens, and puppies.

This was truly a miracle! We all cried for joy and did the happy dance. We would really miss these animals that we had cared for and become attached to, but we had so many empty spaces. We immediately arranged to transfer some animals from LCAS and from the White County animal control.

Three of us from TLC went to make the decisions. It's not an easy thing for any of us to be in the position of making life and death decisions. We have to control our emotions to try to make choices that will be good for the TLC shelter. It's important that we keep our inventory balanced and diverse, and that we not bring back any dogs that would be difficult to adopt. Our space and resources are very limited.

We were also limited in which animals would be available. LCAS is very cost conscious, and restricted us to animals that would probably not be easy for them to adopt. First we took two pregnant dachshund mixes that they couldn't keep and had asked specifically for our help. Then we took a tour of the facility. Some dogs were not available because of temperament, if they had been assessed as aggressive. One dog had killed a lot of chickens, goats, and even an adult deer and he was being held for adoption by a hunter. Some dogs had not passed the required (by law) five day holding period. Lady was the first one they showed us, as she was the most unadoptable dog in their facility because of her age and color. The volunteer had spent some time with her and knew she was a loving dog. We took her for a walk, and as soon as she got out of the cage her tail went up. She responded strongly to the "female touch" that she was offered.

We continued our tour, and made a list of the possible new friends that we might want to bring back. We had already decided that we needed to meet with the Animal Services Committee to discuss each choice, and then we needed to sleep on these choices before we called LCAS to tell them of our decisions.

Lady was at the top of all three of our lists, and was an instant choice. Molly, the middle-aged blue pit bull, was second. She had a very sweet and calm disposition, and blue pit bulls are very popular. The other choice was the only puppy that we were offered, Kelsey. She is a pure bred Red Bone Hound, about four months old. She was extremely skinny. They have a policy of feeding no more than one-half cup of dog food a day to their dogs, regardless of size or age. Kelsey is a very high energy dog and was suffering. The shelter manager did not want us to take her, and said that it meant that he was losing ninety dollars, but the LCAS volunteer helped us to convince him that it would be good for the dog.

LCAS has a shelter manager, two full-time vet techs, and three prison inmates, so it was easy getting the dogs loaded up for their trip to freedom. The paperwork is also easy—we're on the same software system as LCAS so it's an online transfer transaction. Once the papers were signed, we were free to go.

Lady went immediately into a large, grassy, open pen with a dog house full of straw. After the first worries she had about her barking neighbor, she settled in. Our volunteer went right to work to try and find her family. Clearly she was a much loved dog. She called the vet where the tag was registered in 2008 and got the same response that had stymied the LCAS employee. The people had moved and she didn't have current contact information. Unlike LCAS, we're a private agency and not able to obtain the names of the owners. Also unlike the paid employees at LCAS, our volunteer didn't give up. Volunteers tend to be a lot more passionate about these things! The vet's office eventually noticed in the files that they had transferred the records over to another vet! She consented to call the other vet's office, and they had the current information. Within minutes, a very happy man was on the phone asking when he could come to get his dog. What joy! How could it be? The word went around very quickly by way of telephone, emails, and Facebook. We called people we hardly knew to tell them. Some of us even told our dogs this story.

The next day, the happy couple, on their way to pick up their dog, stopped by mistake at LCAS. It's easy to do, since their shelter is less than half a mile away on the same road, and most people don't even realize that there are two shelters. They were greeted by the shelter manager who told them that they had tried to contact them but they never answered. An argument followed, but I wasn't there so I won't comment on that! I did receive a call from the shelter manager to let me know what kind of person the owner was, and that animal control had tried to contact him four times without a response. I asked the owner if that was true and got a very strong answer. That's when he told me about his encounter at LCAS. I am never quick to point fingers, as we all slip up from time-to-time, and I would much rather forgive a mistake than to be told a lie. There is no question that a passionate volunteer will go further to save an animal than a paid employee that's doing a job that is frequently onerous.

The family is happily settling in with their beloved Lady. The children couldn't wait to be reunited with her, and we have since heard from other people how devastated they were when she was lost. They looked for her for a long time, but at 14 years old, finally assumed the worst and ceased to look. She was found miles from her home in an area that no one would have thought to look.

Molly has proven to be the sweet, calm dog that we thought her to be and is in a foster home. Kelsey is in a large pen with lots of toys and a warm bed. She is extremely food aggressive, but we're working on that. It will take some time to fatten her up and convince her that there is plenty of food now.

Old Jack: One Great Hound

Terry Alexander

When I was about ten, my father had a wonderful old black and tan coon dog named Jack. Jack was an amazing dog. Whatever you wanted to hunt, you could just let him smell a pelt of that kind of animal and he would start hunting the animal. He would always hunt until he found one. If you wanted to find a rabbit you could just pull out your lucky rabbit's foot, let Jack smell it, and be guaranteed of finding one. This worked just as well for possums, squirrels, groundhogs, foxes, minks, weasels, or any other kind of animal. Old Jack was one smart dog. He was the only dog I've ever known that had a job.

Back then our next-door neighbor, Tom Holcomb, had a chicken house. He raised chickens to be sold to the market for slaughter. That was a new idea someone had come up with. Well, Mr. Tom would sometimes have dead chickens. He would just toss them out of the chicken house for old Jack. Jack would go up to them, nudge them with his nose, and if they didn't move he would take them away and bury them. If they moved, he would leave them alone. After Mr. Tom saw Jack do this often enough, he just began to let Jack into his chicken house. Jack would then clean out any dead chickens and leave all the live ones alone. So, every morning just before sunrise,

Jack would go through the sowed field, cross the road, go across the four acre patch and go off to work at Mr. Tom's chicken house. When he was finished with work he would come back home. This was a good arrangement for everyone concerned. Jack got all the chicken he could eat. Mr. Tom got his chicken house cleaned out. And we got to brag about having the only dog in the county that had a job.

Jack was the best hunting dog I have ever seen. When he got on the trail of an animal, he wouldn't quit until he had it. One time my friend Cleater and I decided to go coon hunting. Along toward evening we got the coon tail off my dad's car antenna. We let Jack smell it, and he began to get all excited because he knew we were about to go hunting. We got our guns, and off to the woods we went. Jack was running around through the woods hunting coon scent. After about an hour we heard Jack bark, "Oop!" This was the bark he always used to let us know he had found the trail. He would occasionally bark this same bark to let us know he was still on the trail, and to let us know where he was. Every time we heard him bark we ran toward the sound. We were running in the direction of his latest bark, when we heard him bark, "Buuurr!" We knew this bark meant he had treed a coon. We continued to run toward the sound when we heard what sounded like Jack was fighting with something.

I yelled to Cleater, "Reckon what ole Jack's a fightin'?"

Cleater yelled back, "I don't know, but it sounds like it's right over yonder, we'd better get thar quick!"

We approached the area where we thought we had heard the fighting. Everything suddenly became quiet. We both stopped.

Cleater said, "I could ah swore this 'as where Jack was

ah fightin' som'um."

I said, "Me too, but I don't see nothing here."

Cleater said, "Me neither, reckon a bear or pant'er killed 'im and drug 'im off som'ers?"

We both began to frantically yell, "JACK! JACK!" We were really worried about Jack, fearing he had been eaten by something really big. Suddenly, a huge coon dropped out of the big pine tree we were standing under and landed right between us. We both screamed! But that coon just lay there. Then we heard Jack bark. We looked up, and about thirty feet up in that tree was Jack, barking away.

Cleater said, "I knowed ole Jack was the best coon dog in the country, but I never knowed he could climb trees."

I said, "Me neither."

We began to call Jack, "Here boy!" But Jack just stayed up in that tree barking.

Cleater asked, "What we gonna do? I don't think Jack is ever gonna climb down."

I said, "I reckon he can climb up a lot better than he can climb down."

Cleater said, "Yep, I reckon."

We finally decided we would go back to the house and get a rope to rescue him. We thought he might climb down and meet us as we were doing this. But he didn't. When we got back with the rope, he was still up in that tree barking. So we climbed up the tree and lowered him down. After that we always carried a forty feet long rope, with us when we went hunting with ole Jack just in case he decided to climb a tree after something.

Now Jack was not only the best hunting dog around, he was also the best snake dog in the county. One time Cleater and I were playing on the swing set in the yard, when a six foot long timber rattler went slithering across the dirt yard. Back then people had dirt yards. They cleaned them with a hoe so they could see rattle snakes near the house, and because nobody had a lawn mower. I'm not sure if nobody had a lawn mower because nobody could afford one, or because they hadn't been invented yet, or because everybody had dirt yards and didn't need one. Anyway, about the time that snake came slithering across the yard, Uncle Charlie came driving up in his car. He got out of his Ford and started toward the house. Then he saw that rattlesnake.

He yelled at Cleater and me, "Boys, y'all stay put, they's a big ole rattler in the yard!"

So of course we jumped off the swing set and ran toward where Uncle Charlie was yelling.

Uncle Charlie yelled, "I told y'all to stay put!"

I yelled, "Boy at's a big'on' ain't it?"

Cleater yelled, "Yeah, at's the biggest un I ever seen!"

I yelled, "Yep, shore is!"

By now Uncle Charlie was livid. He was yelling, "Ted, you and Cleater stay away from that thang, if it bites ya, it'll kill ya dead!"

Now we weren't as crazy as he seemed to think, we had no intentions of messing with that huge rattlesnake. We just wanted to see it. About this time Jack came out from under the porch to see what all the yelling was about. When he saw that timber rattler he must have thought we were all in trouble because he ran over to it, grabbed the snake's middle with his mouth, and began to shake it back and forth. That snake began to try to bite Jack, and then Jack really began to shake his head fast. Jack was shaking that snake so fast that suddenly we heard a pop, and saw the head of that snake snap off of the snake's body. The snake's mouth was wide open, and the head went straight toward Uncle Charlie. Uncle Charlie was moving backwards really fast when the snake's head hit him. The teeth stuck in! Uncle Charlie rolled up over the hood of his Ford yelling, "Oh, my God, I been bit!"

Cleater and I both began to yell, "Help, help!"

Daddy came running into the yard asking, "What's going on out here?"

By this time Charlie was on the ground yelling, "I been bit, son, I been bit!"

Daddy ran over to him and said, "Let's see how bad it is." He then reached down and pulled off Uncle Charlie's coat. When he did the snake's head was stuck in the coat. Daddy asked, "Where you bit at?"

Uncle Charlie looked down at where the snake's head had hit him, saw the fangs had only stuck into the coat, and said, "Well, dad gommit, so I ain't been bit, but by God I shore have been skeered!"

Daddy walked over to the rattlesnake and cut off the rattles to put in his guitar. It was easy to see Uncle Charlie was a little rattled by the whole experience, so Daddy said, "I recken that'uld ah skeered anybody 'bout to death."

Another time Cleater was over because we were having a hog killing. Every time we killed hogs, while we were cooking down the fat to make lard, we would hear a panther screaming down in the holler below the house. At least we called it screaming, but anyone who has ever heard a panther knows it sounds more like a baby crying really loudly.

Cleater and I had tried to hunt that panther several times, but we only got close enough to catch a glimpse of it one time. We knew if we ever got Jack on its trail that cat was all but done for, but we never had anything for old Jack to smell so he would know he was tracking that panther.

Well, on this day we decided we would go try to shoot that panther again. We got our guns and took off toward that holler. We began to creep out by the old barn so we could get downwind of the panther and sneak up on it. Much to our surprise when we got down to the holler, that big cat was standing there clear as he could be, screaming away. We both began to slowly lift our rifles. That cat must have sensed our presence, because it suddenly glanced toward us and was off like a flash. He ran straight toward the barbed wire fence, went under it and was gone.

Cleater and I were running after it, but we were no match for the speed of that cat. When we got to the fence Cleater said, "Lookie here."

I said, "I'll be dang!" Hanging on one of the barbs of the fence where the panther had gone under it were three dark brown hairs.

We both looked at each other and said, "We got 'im now!" We got the hairs and headed back to get ole Jack.

On the way back I told Cleater, "We better be shore to get the rope, so's we can keep old Jack from climbing the tree a'der 'at ole pant'er."

Cleater said, "Yeah, I reckon we shore had, 'at pant'er might just whoop 'im if 'e gets it cornered."

I said, "Yep."

When we got back to the house, we got the forty-foot rope and called Jack. We let him smell those three hairs, and we were off on the great panther hunt.

Now, that panther was really smart. He went straight for the creek and went down the stream to help wash away the trail. But this didn't slow Jack down very much because he could smell right through the water. We knew he could do this because we had witnessed him follow several old coons who had tried that trick. There was no doubt in our minds that we were going to get us a panther now.

We tracked that cat through briars, creeks, and the swamp behind the house before we finally heard Jack barking that distinctive "Buuurr! Buuurr!" that let us know he had treed that panther. We really began to run harder toward the barking because we knew if Jack climbed that tree he was in for a fight.

When we got there Jack was just about to start climbing the tree. We both ran over to him and got hold of him. We tied that rope around his neck and tied him to a nearby tree. Jack continued to bark at that panther, and the panther sat up in that tree growling at Jack. I looked at Cleater and we both started to slowly raise our rifles. We had that panther just where we wanted it! Slowly we took a bead on that cat. I looked over and Cleater was standing there with his rifle raised, also. We just stood there with our rifles raised.

After what seemed like an eternity Cleater said, "He shore is purdy, ain't 'e?"

I said, "Yeah, he shore is, I ain't never seen ah pant'er up close."

Cleater said, "Me neither, I reckon they ain't many of 'em left anymore."

I said, "Yeah, I reckon they about all been killed out."

Cleater said, "Yep, I reckon so."

I said, "He shore is purty."

Cleater said, "Yep, Let's let 'em go."

I said, "Daddy shore will be mad if 'e ever finds out we had 'im in our sights and let 'im go."

Cleater said, "Well, we'll just say he lost us in the creek." I said, "Daddy knows how good a tracker old Jack is, but he just might buy it."

Cleater said, "Well I don't want to shoot 'em."

I said, "Me neither."

So we both swore we would never tell anyone about letting that panther go. We had to drag Jack away, he couldn't understand what was going on. I finally had to take out my lucky rabbit's foot and let him smell it, so he would catch a rabbit and forget about that panther. When we finally got home and told my dad that the panther had lost old Jack in the creek, my dad gave me that look that said he knew I was not telling the truth. But he never pressed the issue, and I was never more grateful to be let off the hook in my life.

Now, I don't want to give you the wrong impression, we weren't always such good environmentalists. You see, this was back before they had ever invented protecting the environment. We just didn't shoot that Eastern Cougar because it was so rare. But in our defense, we never had any such foolish notions when it came to the alligators! Back when I was growing up, north Georgia had quite a few alligators.

One day Cleater and I were fishing down at the little swamp below the mule barn at my grandfather's farm. We were floating around on a pontoon boat we had made by strapping some empty fifty-gallon barrels to an old sled my grandfather didn't use anymore. Cleater had just caught a brim, and was leaning over to get it in the boat, when a big old fourteen-foot alligator came up out of the water and snapped his jaws together not more than two feet away from Cleater's head. We both screamed!

I said, "Cleater, That old gator almost got your head fer supper!"

Cleater said, "He shore did!" Then he said, "I thank we gonna have to clean the gators out of this swamp before we can fish in it anymore!"

I said, "Yeah, let's go get Jack and see if he can hunt

gators."

Cleater said, "All'ite."

So, we went straight back to the house and got old Jack.

Cleater asked, "How we ever gonna get him to hunt gators? We ain't got nothing fer 'im to smell."

I thought a minute and said, "I thank Daddy's got a gator skin billfold, let's see if he'll let old Jack smell it."

Cleater said, "Yeah, 'at's ah good ide'."

We went and asked my dad if we could let Jack smell his gator skin billfold, so we could go alligator hunting.

My dad said, "Shore, getting rid ah them gators is the best ide' I heared of in a long time. I reckon if any dog can track gators, old Jack can. You know 'e can smell right through water don't ya?" As he said this he looked at me with that knowing look.

I just kind of lowered my head and said, "He shore is a good dog all'ite."

My dad still didn't press the issue about the cougar we had let go. He just took out his wallet and handed it to us. We held that wallet down so Jack could smell it. He instantly began to bark and head off toward the holler. We got our guns and ran after him.

Cleater yelled, "Where's 'e going this ain't toward the swamp."

I yelled, "I'ont know, let's just foller 'im, 'e seems to be on the trail of som'um."

Cleater yelled, "All'ite."

Jack ran straight to the road, stopped and looked both ways (he always did that before he crossed the road) and ran across the road. He then ran straight toward the store. I was thinking that there couldn't be any alligators very close this way. I was wondering if old Jack had finally got on the wrong trail. He had never failed before. I really began to wonder if he had gone crazy when he ran up to the door of E.B. Hunt's store and began to bark, "Buuurr! Buuurr!" just like he had found an alligator in the store.

E.B. stuck his head outside and asked, "What's ole Jack a doing Ted, he's acting like he's got a coon treed.

I said, "Well Barnett, it's like 'is, we 'as gonna go gator hunting so we let 'im smell daddy's billfold to get on the trail of 'em, and he ran off up 'ere. I reckon 'e's gone crazy."

About that time Lenerd Carpenter stuck his head out the door, and he was laughing so hard I was afraid he was going to fall down. Then Lenerd said, "Boys don't y'all know what 'e's ah doing?"

I said, "I recken 'e's gone crazy Lenerd."

Lenerd then said, "Boys 'at dog ain't gone crazy, 'e just smelled the money in Lawrence's billfold and thought 'e'as hunting money. So ah course 'e come up 'ere to the store."

Cleater said, "I reckon that must be hit."

I said, "Yeah, I reckon you got it figured out."

Lenerd said, "That shore is a good dog."

I said, "He's the best!"

We put the rope around Jack's neck and dragged him back to the house. He was barking all the way. I guess he was wondering why we left without any money.

We got back and told my dad about what had happened. He just took the money out of his wallet and said, "Try'is."

He handed his wallet to us and we put it down for old Jack to smell. Jack instantly began to bark and run off toward the swamp. We took off after him. We knew we were on the right trail now. We got onto the pontoon boat and began to pole our way out into the swamp. Jack was just barking away, "Oop, oop!" letting us know he was still on the trail of an alligator. Finally Jack began to bark, "Buuurr, buuurr!" letting us know we were right over one. We threw out the anchor, which was just three fly wheels from some of dad's old junk cars tied together to a plow line.

Then Cleater asked, "How we gonna get that gator to come up so we can shoot 'im?"

I said, "I don't know, boy I wish we had one of them old rotten chickens Jack cleans out of Mr. Tom's chicken house. We could just tie it on this cane pole, dunk it in the water and wait on that gator to come up fer it, and shoot 'im."

Cleater said, "Yeah, that'uld shore be good, but we ain't got no rotten chicken. Heck, we ain't even got nothing that smells like ah old rotten chicken."

Then we both looked at each other and at the same time exclaimed," Our socks!"

So I took one of my socks off, tied it on the cane pole, and dunked it in the water. It wasn't more than two minutes before we were shooting an alligator. By the end of that week we had wiped all the alligators out of that little swamp at my grandfather's farm. We got eight in all out of it. We also took Jack all around the swamp and let him find all the alligator eggs. And there hasn't been an alligator in it since.

Now, my dad was so proud of us cleaning all the alligators out of the swamp he began to brag to all the neighbors about how we could go swimming in the swamp now and not have to worry about getting eaten. Soon the neighbors began to ask us to come clean all the gators out of their swamps. Cleater and I had a pretty good business going there for about two summers. We would wait until Jack got off work and head over to whatever neighbor needed their swamp or pond cleaned and get alligators. The neighbors would feed us and we got to keep the hides. You could get a dollar each for them, and back then a dollar was a lot of money for a ten year old. But after about two summers we had wiped all the alligators out of north Georgia. We did such a good job there hasn't been an alligator spotted in north Georgia since.

Well, one day we were eating supper when we heard a knock at the door. My dad got up to go see who it was.

Then he yelled out, "Ted, they's ah game warden here to see ya!"

Now I was really worried, I was afraid he might be mad about us killing all the alligators in north Georgia." I thought he might be here to arrest me. We were always a bit leery of game wardens. I slowly moved to the door and said, "Yes'ir?"

He looked at me and asked, "Is you one ah dem boys theys call the gator hunters?"

I don't know why, but I began to start talking really fast, "Yes'ir, but I didn't know they's nothing wrong with killing gators. Everbody's real happy to have 'um gone, I thought they's just a pest, and they's dangerous too. They could eat a little kid, or a dog, or som'rn. They weren't no good fer nothing. Honest, I didn't know you couldn't kill 'em. Please don't take me to jail. Please don't."

Then he said, "Wow, slow down boy, I ain't here to take ye to jail. The government heared about ya killin' all the gators out of north Georgia, and them folks in Atlanter told me to come see if we could hire y'all out fer the summer so's ya could wipe out the gators in South Georgia."

I said, "They want to hire us?" He said, "Yep, five dollars a day each, and you keep the hides."

I said, "I'ont know, it sounds real good but they's ah few problems. First it 'uld have to be all'ite with me and Cleater's folks. Second, well we could never get all them gators without ole Jack to track 'em, and Jack has a job cleaning out Mr. Tom's chicken house every morning And third, I don't know where we'uld stay at in south Georgie."

The game warden said, "We done worked all that out, I talked to your and Cleater's daddys, you will be staying in cabins at state parks, and the state will send a man to clean out the chicken house for Jack. I know Jack gets paid in chickens, and the state will be paying him five dollars a day to so you will be able to buy him all the chicken he wants. Now you boys knows what a pest them gators is, and it's your duty to help get rid of 'em."

I said, "Well I reckon we'll try."

So the next day Jack, Cleater and I were in a state van heading south. Well, we did pretty well for the first month. We wiped all the gators out of most of Georgia, but then they moved us to the Okeefenokee swamp. I couldn't believe it when I saw it.

I said, "Cleater, you ever seen anythang like 'is?"

Cleater said, "Naw, this swamp is bigger than Lake Lanier."

I said, "Yep, and it took us over a month to clean the gators out of the lake."

Cleater asked, "Reckon we'll ever be able to catch all the gators out'a here?"

I said, "I 'ont know, but it's our duty to try. If we can get them gators out a here they might be able to drain this thang and turn it into som'um useful.

"Cleater said, "Yep that shore would be good."

We only had about two months left until we had to start back to school. Well, we gave it our best shot, but we probably didn't even kill a third of the gators in that swamp. Then we had to go back to school.

The next summer we went back and it was like we had never started because the young ones had hatched. We killed alligators all summer and still didn't get half of them. We went back the next summer and took one look, I think there were more alligators in the swamp than when we started.

We went to the game warden and told him we didn't think there was any use trying, because there just wasn't enough time in the summer to get all the alligators. We told him we would be glad to come back and wipe them out after we graduated school. But we never did get the chance to do that, because by the time we had graduated school, conservation had been invented and the government had decided alligators were a good thing. That, and by the time we had graduated, old Jack had gotten killed. That's why there are still alligators in South Georgia.

As I've said before Jack was an amazing dog. Not only was he the only dog I've ever known that had a job, able to climb trees like a cat, and the best hunting dog I've ever seen, he was also the oldest dog I've ever heard of.

My dad always said that as best he could estimate Jack was thirty-two years old when he was killed. I've heard it said that for every year a dog lives it is like seven years to a human. So if Jack was thirty two in human years, in dog years he would have been UH, UH, UH, really old. I was really puzzled the day I found old Jack dead. He had been run over by a car, and he always looked both ways before he crossed the road.

The day began like any other. We ate breakfast, and Jack headed off to work. He always came back home by nine, but that day it got to be noon and I still hadn't seen Jack since breakfast. So I went to look for him, when I got to the road I saw him and began to cry. From the mess in the road there was no doubt what had happened. I ran home to tell my dad.

Dad wiped a tear from his eye and said, "Well, I'll take care of burying him, why don't you go tell Tom that Jack won't be cleaning out his chicken house anymore."

I said, "All'ite." I went the long way around, so I didn't have to see Jack like he was. I got to Mr. Tom's house and knocked on the door. When Mr. Tom came out I started to cry again and said, "Old Jack got run over, he's dead! I don't understand it, he always looked both ways before he crossed the road.

"Mr. Tom said, "Oh no, it might be my fault.

I said, "What?"

Mr. Tom said. "Come 'ere."

We walked around the house, and there in a new dog pen was a female black and tan hound dog. Mr. Tom said, "I got her hoping I could breed her to Jack and get some pups like him. She was cutting up yesterday and I put Jack in with 'er. I guess when he left this morning his mind just wasn't on the road."

I said, "I guess not, at least not 'til that car hit 'im!"

P.S. Several months later Mr. Tom came by with a black and tan puppy with a ring around his neck. Ring was the best dog I ever owned!

If your pet could talk, what would it say?

Thank you to the students of Mrs. Dicken's 2nd Grade.

Bear Facts

Mary Ellen Moore

Bear, a mixed Lab, was quite possibly the smartest dog I've ever known. When he wanted to cross the street, he stopped, looked both ways, and then crossed safely. He went to town every day and made his rounds so faithfully that people began referring to him as "the town mayor." Almost everybody in town knew and loved him. He knew that the cafe on the corner saved some bacon just for him. He liked to nap on the second floor of a shop in town but arose to greet all customers. He rarely barked and caused no problems.

Bear became my dog by default. My son Christopher, who was about to go off to college, brought home a fuzzy little white puppy with a black nose. He named him "Bear" because he said he looked like a polar bear. Christopher soon went off to college, and Bear was a wonderful companion to me for almost twenty-two years.

I had a small shop in my small town for several years, and Bear would "keep shop" with me every day. Customers came more to see him than to shop. Sometimes he went to visit the lady in the shop next door to mine. One late afternoon as I was closing my shop, Bear went next door to visit without my knowledge. He quietly settled down without the shop keeper knowing he was there.

She closed her store for the day as I locked mine, and we both left.

When I reached my home five minutes away, Bear was not there to greet me, but I didn't worry because I knew he was around somewhere and would be home in time for supper. Little did I know that he had been locked in the shop next door to mine. He didn't panic; he just made himself at home by jumping on the quilt display and settling in for a long nap. A neighbor who drove past the shop later told me that he seemed perfectly at home sleeping on the quilt in the front window. He didn't seem to mind that he had made himself comfortable on a five-hundred-dollar display in the front window of a downtown shop. It wasn't until the next morning that someone called to tell me that Bear was on display. The next day the shopkeeper was very gracious, but after that we both made sure of Bear's whereabouts before locking up!

Stilt-Walker

Lynda Holmes

Your cat is hiding from my dog:
She climbed the tallest tree.
We hate it when she does that
'Cause we have to set her free.
We used to solve the problem
With a ladder from my Dad,
Although he wasn't very happy,
And it didn't make him glad.

Must Love Dogs

Sudie Crouch

Usually, when couples tell the story of how they met, it's something along the lines of they were set up on a blind date, introduced by friends, or met at school or work. When people ask my husband, Lamar, and me how we met, we answer, "Venus". We usually get a chuckle, as if we are referring to the mystical, mythological goddess of love who brings soul mates together. In actuality, we are referring to Venus, our female German Shepherd, who is closer to the Great Houdini when to it comes to escaping than any mythological love goddess.

I was working for Clinique and my now mother in law, Gladys, worked for Estee Lauder. Despite being competitors on the sales floor, we were close friends. One morning, as we headed to the floor, Joni, another salesperson, came in, eyes wide and a terrified look on her face. When asked what was wrong, she replied, "I just had a German Shepherd chase me all the way out of our subdivision." Joni lived two streets over from Gladys.

"A German Shepherd? Was he okay?" Gladys asked.

Joni nodded. "He seemed okay, he seemed like he was trying to get in my car."

Gladys nodded, adding, "Well, hopefully his owner will come home and get his dog soon."

When Joni walked off, Gladys grabbed my arm in what I have come to call her Death Grip and said in a whisper, "That's my son's dog."

"Your son's dog?" I asked.

"Yes, he's out of town doing some work for his sister and he left that fool dog with me." She shook her head, her blonde curls bouncing, "I hope that dog doesn't bite anyone, I don't want to be sued."

Later that evening, Gladys frowned and said, "I really hope nothing happens to that dog. Lamar will kill me."

"Why did your son leave him with you, anyway?" I asked.

"He left the dog for his brother, Shonn, to watch and when Shonn let the dog out to feed him, the dog escaped and he has been loose ever since."

"How long has that been?" I asked. Gladys thought for a second, "It was the first day Lamar left, so . . . five days?"

"Gladys!" I exclaimed. "Okay, I will come over to your house when we get off and get that dog up," I offered.

Gladys looked at me from head to toe, all decked out in my Clinique lab coat and heels and frowned, "You? What do you know about dogs?" she asked.

I laughed. "I am an old country girl and come from a long line of dog charmers. I'll have that dog up in no time."

That evening, I followed Gladys home to execute Operation Dog Rescue. When I got out of my car, I saw the dog, a smaller sized German Shepherd, sitting at the corner of Gladys' front yard.

"What's the dog's name?" I asked.

"His name is Venus," Gladys told me.

"Gladys, he is a SHE if the name is Venus."

"Either way, I don't think you are going to be able to get her up," she said. "I am going in the house to get a leftover hamburger, maybe you can lure her with that."

I asked Gladys where the kennel was and she directed

me to the back yard. "Be careful," Gladys warned, "she may bite you, she has tried to bite Shonn."

I just shook my head. "Venus!" I said sternly. "Come!" By some grace of a miracle, or maybe Venus knew she was in the presence of a dog charmer, she got up and walked alongside me, straight to her kennel. There was no barking, no biting, no signs of some vicious, rabid German Shepherd. Just a few courtesy licks and nudges of my hand to scratch behind her ears. Gladys emerged from her back deck, hamburger patty in one hand, flashlight in the other, focusing the beam right in my face.

"Careful, Sudie, she's gonna eat you up," she warned.

"Gladys, put that thing away. I am more worried about stepping on a snake than this dog biting me."

I fixed the lock the best I could with a face full of flashlight blinding me and we went into the house for a few minutes.

"I have to call Lamar," she said, picking up the phone. "Son, it's your mother," she announced, "I wanted to tell you, your dog is fine. My friend, Sudie, came over tonight and finally got him back up. Her. Whatever it is. Here—tell her thank you."

She thrust the phone to me. The first words my husband ever said to me were: "Thank you. Now, please put my mother back on the phone." I handed the phone back to Gladys.

She was silent for a second, then said, "Lamar, darlin', I never lied to you, I knew she was ok, I could see her chasing cars from the kitchen window every evening . . ."

Venus, the Houdini German Shepherd, really is the goddess of love. Because of her escape from the woman who would become my mother in law, I really did meet my true love.

Horses Are Intelligent and Loving

Robbie Niles

In my opinion, horses are the most misunderstood creatures. Historically, we hear of horses being mastered by frightening them senseless, bronco-busted, broken, whipped, and on and on. It breaks my heart to know what pain and suffering is still being imposed on these shy, gentle, intelligent creatures by some people out of sheer ignorance.

It has been my experience that horses try very hard to do what they think we want them to do. It is we who are to blame for not being able to communicate with them on the level we both can understand; not brute force, but common, ordinary thought—telepathy—and gentleness.

I first encountered a reference to our telepathic connection with horses when I read "Horses are Made to be Horses" by Franz Mairinger, a Spanish Riding School instructor for many years.

He tells about when he was the student learning to ride the fabulous Lipizzaner of the Spanish Riding School. His instructor told him to concentrate on getting to the middle of the ring and performing his task (the levade) and getting back out, and to be very careful not to worry about anything else, like hoping that the horse would wait until he got to the center before performing his task.

Mairinger said that as he was riding down the side of the ring to the spot where he was supposed to turn into the center, he thought just what the instructor had warned him not to think, and, to his horror, the horse stopped right there and did the levade.

He then had to proceed on into the middle of the ring and do it again. He said his horse was not at all happy with him for having to do his task twice.

My next exposure to the concept was when my riding instructor told me to drop the reins, relax, and picture in my mind the horse walking to a certain post and stopping there. Then to picture—in my mind only—the horse starting. Then sit quietly. No body movement. No weight-shifting. No movement at all. It happened precisely as I had pictured it in my mind. The horse walked to the post and stopped. Wow.

Here are a couple of wonderful stories about some of my best friends.

I Change My Mind

About a half-mile from the house, heading home at the end

of a pleasant trail ride on my lovely white mare, Amarito, I decided to take a detour to check on some azalea plantings before ending our ride. We had never done that before.

I thought for a while about where the best place would be to turn into the woods to get to the azaleas. Then, after making the decision, my thoughts wandered on to things totally unrelated to riding a horse.

After about ten minutes, we approached the planned turn-off, and at the last minute, I decided that the leaves and pine-straw would make the footing too slippery for Amarito's iron shoes, so decided not to visit the azaleas after all.

Apparently Amarito didn't catch my last-minute change of plans, because she turned into the woods at the exact spot I had pictured in my mind. She had read my mind.

Thank You, Girls

At one time there was a small herd of pleasure horses at my barn. They had free access to the barn, the pasture, and the road leading to the barn. Their boundaries were set by electric fences.

One day I was working on an electric fence when my pliers accidently touched the live wire. There was a loud crack as the electricity traveled through the pliers to my fingers. I yelped and fell over backwards, landing on my rear end. I was shaken, but not hurt. I decided that I must be getting tired, so I should call it a day and return to the house.

I noticed that two of the mares who had been hanging around watching me work had moved closer while I was sitting on the ground, but thought nothing of it. Then, as

I got to my feet and started walking up the road to the house, the mares positioned themselves on either side of me with their shoulders softly brushing my shoulders. I was astounded. Awed. They were very gently supporting me. They were not being pushy—just there in case I stumbled.

I stopped and turned to these lovely creatures and thanked them for their help, but assured them that I could make it on my own. I gave them both a good scratch behind the ears and a pat on the neck, and started up the road again.

But they ignored my protestations of good health and fitness. They again positioned themselves as before, and gently escorted me all the way to the gate.

Lost and Found ... an Unsolved Mystery

Susan S. Dodds

For a number of years we lived four miles outside of town off of a well-traveled highway. One Saturday evening, while on my way to shop in town, I noticed an abandoned car at the edge of the highway near our subdivision. I finished shopping and while returning home, noticed the same car still there. I thought perhaps someone needed help, since seeing a car on the side of the highway near our home was highly unusual. As I drove slowly by the car, I did not notice anyone in it. Just to be safe I had my daughter, who was with me, jot down the tag number. As I passed the car, I noticed something white a few feet in front of the car on the shoulder of the road. My daughter screamed, "Mom, it's a cat!" Fearful that the poor little thing could become road kill at any second, I braked the car and my daughter jumped out and scooped up the frightened little fur ball.

Once home, we took a good look at the cat. She had just a little bob of a tail. She had unusually soft fur (unlike any I had ever seen on a cat). She also had an unusual stance . . . her back legs seemed smaller than her front. Assuming that the cat belonged to the owner of the abandoned vehicle on the highway, I dialed 911. In my best heroine voice I announced to the officer who answered the phone, that I was reporting an abandoned vehicle and proudly gave the color, make and tag of the car. I then went on to say that there was no one in the car when I drove by, but that his or her cat had obviously gotten out of the vehicle and I had rescued it. I gave my name, number and hung up, pleased with myself that the owner would be calling me soon.

About an hour later, my good friend, Brenda called. She was on the local police force. Her first words were, "Only you would call 911 about a cat!" Taken aback, I asked what she was talking about. It seems that she was in the room when my 911 call came through. She had immediately jumped into action, had tracked down the owner of the vehicle and she had something to report to me. She then said that the owner of the car was a teenager who lived in another part of the county. He had been on his way to his girlfriend's house, had run out of gas and had walked to her house several miles away. When my friend, the police officer, asked him about the cat I had found, he scoffed that it was not his, and that he "hated cats".

Even though it was a weekend my daughter and I immediately went into action. OK, so the cat did not belong to the owner of the car on the highway. There were no houses near where we found her. Our subdivision was a good half mile off the highway. I was sure though, that somehow the cat had gotten away from its owner somewhere in the subdivision. We made all kinds of phone calls to neighbors, made posters and posted them all around the subdivision and on telephone poles up and down the highway. We made sure that our message was simple and the lettering large enough to be read by anyone driving by. (I have noticed that so many people do not think about this and make their message for a lost animal too small to be seen well from the road.) Nothing came of our efforts. First thing Monday morning I put an ad in the paper under Lost and Found, posted notices at all the local vets and at the local shelter. Two weeks later with no calls in response to our notices, we decided we had a new addition to our family. We had already named her Bunni, because of her short, fluffy bob of a tail (similar to a rabbit's tail). I took her to a vet for her physical and shots. After being checked by the doctor, he announced that she was approximately six months old and already spayed. Then, to my surprise, told me that she was a Japanese Bob Tail, a rather rare breed of cat. I have always had cats and must admit that I had never heard of this particular breed. When I looked up the breed in one of my 'cat books' my heart skipped a beat. There was our Bunni, identical in the picture to the real thing. We continued to post notices, make phone calls and run ads for another month . . . even though we had already accepted the little girl into our home and hearts. No one ever responded. I think we did everything that one could possibly do when finding a lost pet. So we took the next step, we made her a part of our family. She is still with us fifteen years later, a little deaf but still beautiful and sweet and such a joy in our lives. I wish her first owner could know that she is loved.

My Earliest Memory of a Dog

Emily Lewy

Frank was Grandpa's dog. My memories of him are through the eyes of a child, for both Frank and Grandpa crossed the Rainbow Bridge when I was only six years old.

Frank was big for a dog. As I remember, he stood about as tall as me. He had thick, fuzzy, yellow fur. No doubt about it, he was Grandpa's dog, but he did like me. I remember hugging him a lot.

My favorite memory was Frank and me riding in the car with Grandpa and Grandma the time we stopped alongside the road near a creek on Grandpa's farm.

The four of us walked through the woods to a perfect spot along the creek. It was beautiful. The flowing water was clear as glass. Moss and ferns growing in the shade along the creek made the area a wondrous, almost magical place.

Grandma showed me how to scoop up cool water with my hands. We all drank from the creek. And then, Grandpa suggested that I follow Frank into the creek.

Wading in the creek with Frank is one of my all-time favorite memories. The water was not too deep and with Frank by my side, it was great fun to gently splash the water.

Time is lost in this childhood memory. Grandma and Grandpa could have watched Frank and me in that creek for only minutes or maybe for a long time. I do not know. But the memory of wading with Frank is as real and wonderful today as it was the day it happened.

Happy Rescue Story: Princess Leia was rescued from a local animal shelter and now lives with a loving family in Florida.

Corkie, the Dog Who Could Spell

Sue Gay

Corkie was a border collie-terrier mix, abused and thrown away. By the time we saw him, he was a bright-eyed, playful and loving puppy who had been nourished and nurtured with good food, vitamins and love by a caring vet, so Corkie could become healthy enough for adoption. One look and we were goners. Corkie came home with us.

Corkie's propensity for getting into trouble was matched only by his seeming need to confess his misdeeds; perhaps the result of his upbringing in heavily Catholic New Mexico. Corkie would greet us at the door emitting a mixture of pathetic howls and whines and we knew to look for trouble. It wasn't hard to find. He made no attempt to cover his tracks. Once he snatched a rhubarb-strawberry pie off the kitchen counter and carried it to the center of my bed. He proceeded to make a mess and then left it. Apparently, rhubarb was not to his liking. Then there was the time he got the plastic lid off a large can of broccoli-cheddar cheese soup mix and ate the whole thing. That was very much to his liking.

Perhaps one of the most memorable things about Corkie was his high degree of intelligence. He quickly learned what certain words meant. "Walk" was his favorite. His ears would perk up and he would run to the door barking for his walk. For our own protection, we started spelling W-A-L-K, even in casual conversation. After what seemed an inordinately short period of time, Corkie would hear W-A-L-K and his ears would perk up and he would run to the door barking, ready for his walk. When I related this to my mother, she looked skeptically at me and said "Are you telling me that dog can spell?" Well, yes, I guess I was. Corkie had learned to spell.

Rest in peace, Corkie.

Sasha, the Amazing Cat

Emily Lewy

Many years ago the last of our cats had crossed the Rainbow Bridge and our home seemed empty without the purring and presents that can only be provided by a cat.

I called Roxy, a very nice young woman I had met at a TLC meeting to find out where we might find a new kitten. Back in those days our county had no animal shelter and TLC, the humane society, operated only with foster homes.

Roxy gave me the phone number of a friend who had a couple of young kittens in her barn. And that is where we found Sasha, an adorable orange kitty.

The first night we placed her in a box since a barn kitty would certainly not be housebroken. When she immediately climbed out, we covered the box with a weighted down wire rack to keep her safe for the night. The next morning, we wakened to find her prancing around the house. This was one tough little kitty with a mind of her own.

She learned to use the doggie door right away. No litter box for her. In no time at all, she was bringing in presents of mice and voles. For fifteen years she had my husband wrapped around her little paw. He adored that cat.

Sasha was such an athletic creature that vets expressed amazement at her muscular physique and made comments about her looking like a boy. Although she was taken to the vet more than once due to her adventurous exploits, she was smart enough to cross the street by walking through the open sewer to the other side.

But one Sunday evening around nine o'clock, she came inside with her lower jaw broken and hanging and her right leg smashed. Sasha was so badly damaged that we did not expect her to survive.

The most wonderful vet ever agreed to meet us at her office. This woman was new to the practice and I had never met her before. She had me hold Sasha for her to take x-rays. The leg was crushed. She feared the leg might have to be amputated, but she would try to save it if that was what we wanted. Of course, we would not want to cramp Sasha's style!

The next day, we brought Sasha home with a jaw wired together and wearing a pink, green and white cast on her leg. This most amazing cat could not be stopped. She was running around and eating solid food in no time. We heard the clomp, clomp of the cast as she climbed the stairs for several weeks, but the leg was saved and the jaw fully recovered.

We were never sure what had happened to cause so much damage. The vet thought she had been knocked down and rolled under a car.

Sasha continued to be a very active for many years. She brought adventure and excitement to our lives.

If your pet could talk, what would it say?
Thank you to the students of Mrs. Dicken's 2nd Grade.

Tally

Brenda P.

Our family was heartbroken when our fifteen-year-old beagle, named Rebel, died. We received many kind, supportive words from other animal lovers, but one comment stuck in our heads. A stranger that we happened to talk to about losing our dog told us that our next dog would find us. We didn't think too much about the comment then, but through life's series of circumstances it came true.

We decided that we would wait awhile before getting a new dog. We needed time to grieve and process the loss. We thought we might be ready after the holidays. On January 8, 2009 one of our sons proclaimed that was the day we needed to go look for our new family member at the Lumpkin County Georgia Animal Shelter. After school and work, we eagerly piled into the car and raced down to the shelter only to arrive after the shelter had closed. The last remaining staff member was locking the door when we walked up. Instead of turning us away so she could go home, she told us if there was a chance we would adopt a dog she would stay and let us in. As soon as we walked in the front office we all glanced down a short hallway to an open door and there, high up in a kennel was the face of puppy love at first sight and she was staring at us! We forced ourselves to go look at all the adult dogs before we went to investigate that face responsible for the magical impression she made on all of us. There were so many beautiful adult dogs all looking anxiously at us. It brought tears to our eyes to see so many deserving animals. We wanted to take them all. We finally walked into the puppy room to get a close up look at that tiny, eight-week-old, four-pound pup. She looked mostly beagle but her facial features were a little finer than a beagle puppy. We quickly looked at all the other puppies in the room and rushed back to her. It was not necessary to have a family discussion about our choice. She came home with us that night. She was scared. She had been picked up as a stray that young. I'm sure her short eight week life had been pretty rough but we gained her trust quickly. We had read the books that say to crate your puppy and not to have them in your bed at night. Those books must have been written by the same authors that say your babies shouldn't sleep in the parental bed either. So the first whimper on the third night had my husband busting Tally out of her jail cell and hoisting her up on

our bed where she curled up between us and we all fell asleep with smiles on our faces.

Tally grew and gained weight and turned into what looks like and acts like a beautiful, smart, twenty-pound, brown-and-white Beagle/Jack Russell mix. You can pick out the Beagle and the Jack characteristics both physically and by behavior. She tracks like a Beagle but she is silent like a Jack. She is active, alert and in charge like a Jack, demanding many walks a day but she can be as lazy as an old hound. Once it gets dark or if the weather isn't perfect, she wants to curl up, preferably on someone's lap or in someone's bed for a good long nap. She has a silky coat like a Beagle, but she never smells "doggie".

Everything in life is controlled by time and circumstance. That stranger who told us our next dog would find us was right. All we had to do was follow the leads we were given. We went to the shelter that day and luckily ran into that caring shelter staff member working that day who allowed us in after hours so Tally could find us.

The Drop-Off

Dr. Bill Haney

It was a brisk autumn morning in late October. The fall leaves had just started to blanket the driveway and the coolness in the air allowed us to keep the windows open that finally let the fresh air into our log home. Once again, the weather was livable after a record-setting long hot summer. The color on Wauka Mountain was absolutely fabulous as each one of the trees displayed its collective greatness of nature.

Our family finally had a day of rest after celebrating another exciting "Gold Rush Days" weekend in Dahlonega with friends who flew in from Florida to see the colorful foliage. So, sleeping in late that morning was the only thing on my mind. Life was certainly sweet that morning.

That morning slumber was shattered by Max barking up a storm downstairs. I shouted, "Max, shut up! I'm sleeping!" But Max continued her barking, followed by the whining that indicated to all of us that something was "out there."

Yellow Labs are certainly noted for their protective nature toward their family, or at least Max was to our family. She is not only a great watch dog but also a barky nuisance when she wants to alert us to anything out of the norm on the property . The alarm bark does not happen too often, but when it does, we pay attention to it.

Max came to us from the local rescue league. She was a shy and formally abused puppy, but after we adopted her she quickly became a loving member of the family. And she knows that she is "queen" of the house! She also knows her barking would be paid attention to every time.

I finally got up to see what the racket was all about. I put my robe on, stumbled downstairs, and walked up to Max staring out the front door. Her tail was pointed straight out indicating she had made contact with "the enemy." But when I approached her she started to wag her devilish yellow tail wanting me to play with her and her favorite ball. I know what the game was . . . it was the "I-wake-you- up- and-you-play-with-me-game." I wasn't buying it.

I looked out the front door and saw nothing. I looked down at Max and saw a slobbery old tennis ball in her mouth. "It's nothing but a stupid squirrel," I yelled to her assuming another squirrel just passed across the front porch. I shook my head, and wandered into the kitchen to pour some orange juice. No use going back to sleep now.

"Max, you are a barky thing! Don't you pay attention to the day! It's Saturday which means SLEEP day." I growled at her, and she did nothing but wag her tail. I scooped out her measured food into the bowl and she started her morning snack. I sipped my orange juice and stared out at the driveway admiring the leaves.

As I glanced out the front window, something caught my eye. It darted from tree to tree slowly approaching the house. I glanced over at Max still gobbling down her food. I turned again to the outside and saw it clearly. As I walked toward the front window a black and white cat was walking toward the house. I had never seen this cat before in the area. I had seen all sorts of cats, but never a black and white one so beautiful.

Slowly she approached, stealthily but with certainty. But something was certainly different about this cat. It looked different. I got closer to the window because something did not look right. Finally, after she made her way up the walkway close enough I deciphered what was different about this cat.

In her mouth, held carefully by the scruff of the neck, was a kitten. It was so small that it could hardly be distinguished. She looked up at the house, and saw me in the window staring her down. I did not move. It was a show-down: eyeball to eyeball. She was frozen in her tracks trying to figure out her next move. And so was I.

Then something extraordinary happened. She bravely approached the house, walked up to the very front steps and let go of the prize in her mouth. The kitten dropped to the stair with a gentle thud, and mother cat looked at me one more time.

All I could think of at that point was Max rushing up to the front door and barking her head off scaring everyone to death. But instead, as if guided by a quieting hand, Max looked out the front door and did nothing. No hairs on her back were raised and no utterance from her mouth came out. We both stared at the beautiful little kitten.

The mother cat gave her kitten on last lick and then turned around and walked back up the driveway disappearing into the trees.

Max and I were stunned. We turned and looked at each other and then turned back to the helpless kitten. He was sitting there, looking at the front door, eeking out the slightest "meow." I had no idea what to do. But I did know that the large lug Max wanted to get to the kitten not to hurt him, but to sniff and get to know the new creature now living on the front step. I could not imagine the fear that this kitten would have to see eighty pounds of "Max" bolting at him from the front door.

I coaxed Max into another room and closed the door. She let out a bark that clearly admonished me for not letting her become part of "the action." I slowly and quietly opened the front door and made my way to the kitten.

He was beautiful. He looked just like his momma. He was a black cat but with strategically placed white markings on his paws and face. A beautiful blaze of white adorned his chest. And he had a gentle and loving voice as he "meowed" from his perch.

I was not sure what to do. I never owned a cat in my life. I had hardly ever been around cats. In fact, I was not a "cat person." I preferred the company of dogs that came when I called them and who played rough and "manly" with tug-toys and tennis balls. So my first instinct was to collect this kitten and take him to the local animal shelter where he could be adopted by a nice "cat family."

I inched toward the kitten. And just as I got to him he darted under the wood porch steps just out of reach. "Come here little kitty . . . come here," I uttered. What a dunce! Cats don't come when called! I tried again and again to reach under the porch, but he would not come out.

I went back into the house and decided to lure him out with warm milk, just like the stereotypical procedure calls for. I place the milk on the step and waited patiently. Nothing happened. Finally, I gave up walking into the house frustrated. Max wondered where her prize was and

I simply pointed out the front door where she stood guard for any signs of the kitten. I carried on my morning activity like nothing had happened.

As the family started to wake, I forgot to tell them about the kitten. So when Max was let loose out front for her morning walk and "ball throw" she immediately fixated on the bowl of milk gobbling up every last drop. My spouse, pointing at the empty milk bowl, yelled, "What's this for?"

The story was explained as the kitten under the steps started to "meow." The quest was now on to capture kitty! Renewed in my quest to make sure he lived, I scrambled up some eggs and put them on the steps again in the same place as the milk. I waited. And then slowly, the kitten came out and began to lick the eggs waiting for him in the bowl.

I did nothing except stare at him. I could feel my emotions well up inside me about this abandoned, orphaned kitty. He was no bigger than the palm of my hand. He looked so helpless. I let him eat what he wanted and then he darted back under the steps. It looked like he found a new home.

Later in the day I made more scrambled eggs for him and he ate them up. This process continued for two more days as generally he gained courage to come closer and closer to me. On the third morning I reached out and grabbed him and put him in my lap. He sat there looking up at me completely trusting me with his future. I brought him inside and introduced him to Max for the first time. Strangely, he was not afraid of big old Max. And in fact, kitty cuddled up to Max as if to gain some warmth from her thick coat of fur. Max looked dumfounded at me. Trying to play "hard to get," Max walked away from kitty as her new friend followed her all around the house.

I scooped kitty up and decided that he was going to a part of the family. Even though I had never owned a cat before, I knew that it was no coincidence that this beautiful creature was dropped off on my front steps. And it was my responsibility to love and nurture him forever. I noticed he was nibbling on my finger, sometimes pinching me hard. "Fang! I'll name you Fang! That's it! That's a cute cuddly name for a kitty!"

Fang has since become a loyal member of the family growing with us over the past two years. Taking his cues from Max, Fang has learned to come when I call him. Honestly, he thinks he is a dog! Max and him play together now and even sleep next to one another. Fang's personality is what I cherish the most. He helps me work on my computer every morning, sorts papers for me on my desk, and even helps tidy up the kitchen . . . all in his own "special" way. He cuddles up to me when I watch TV in the evening, and even greets me along with Max every day when I come home from work in the evening.

I love Fang, my first cat. And his momma who came to our house that October morning has the satisfaction of knowing that she chose a house to bring her kitten to that would take care of him all the days of his life! Thanks for the package, momma!

Just A Dog

Sudie Crouch

It was the first day of summer, 2008. Our eldest Shepherd, Comet, went on over the Rainbow Bridge. I remember that night as if it were yesterday, the lump forming in my throat, the tears pooling in my eyes before they run down my face, that familiar ache in my chest around my heart. I remember taking my son, Cole, to school two days later, in a fog from crying for over forty-eight hours straight, and telling his teacher, Miss Kenia, what happened. I somehow managed to get through the day.

When I went to pick Cole up, another parent asked me what had made him so upset. "Comet died this weekend", I told her. "Comet?" she asked. "Our dog, our oldest." She laughed, and said "Oh girl, it was just a dog, I thought it was something important."

I know that there are, sadly, many people who look on pets as "just a dog" or "just a cat" or "just a fish" or whatever animal form we have chosen to love. But Comet was by no means, just a dog. He was a noble creature that had been by husband's side for nearly thirteen years. This dog was the one that, when young, Lamar would take to the park to train, and the K-9 officers would pull over, get out of their car and watch . . . master and canine. When my friend Renee's husband, Andy, saw him for the first time, he was in awe. "He's the King. That's the King right there and he knows it," Andy announced.

He was a larger Shepherd, blonde and black and one of the most noble looking dogs I have ever seen. It was like you could just see this dog's character. Comet definitely was an impressive looking animal.

Comet tolerated me really well. I remember the first time I baby talked him, and said "Does Comet want a bone?" in a high pitched voice. I got 'the look' and Lamar shook his head.

"He hates baby talk, wouldn't allow it when he was a puppy, won't stand for it now. He wouldn't even let me kiss him when he was a puppy. It made him mad. Comet is not a love dog, he is all about business."

I quit talking baby talk to Comet, and was surprised when he would come up, when no one else, let alone the rest of the pack, was around. He would nudge me, wanting me to pet him, the no love dog, wanting love.

When I was pregnant with my son, Cole, I developed carpal tunnel so horribly in my left hand, that I could not sleep. I would lie on the couch, my left arm hanging down, crying softly because it hurt so badly. Suddenly, I would feel a furry head nudge my hand that was hanging down, and Comet would be crawling beside the couch, positioning himself to where his head was right under my hand, to prop it up. It was like he knew that my hand would feel better being propped up, and maybe the pain was relieved from being elevated, or maybe it was because it was resting on Comet's head.

Then once Cole was born, he had terrible colic for weeks. I was up with him, sometimes all night. Comet was right there with us.

I hate to be tickled, and one night when Cole was a few

months old, Lamar decided to grab me and tickle me. I was screaming, telling him to stop. Lamar stopped when he felt Comet's mouth grab hold of his arm. Comet didn't turn loose until Lamar let me go. Lamar was his owner, his guardian, but somewhere during our journey, Comet had discovered that he not only loved Lamar but me as well.

This dog, who didn't like being kissed or loved on, also let Cole do all of those things to him. When Cole was around eighteen months old, he toddled over to where Comet was lying in front of the gas stove, spread his blue blankie on top of the giant dog, and laid down on top of him. Comet just smiled.

Where he normally would forcefully take a piece of meat out of your hand, he was extra gentle when Cole offered him a chicken finger he wanted to share. Cole could grab him on both sides of his head and kiss Comet squarely on the nose. Comet showed a love to our son that was remarkable and beyond anything we expected. If you raised your voice at Cole, you got a stern reprimanding bark with 'the look' that you needed to take it down a notch. And Cole felt a love for Comet, smiling so bright and big when he'd put his tiny arm around Comets massive neck.

The last two years of Comet's life, he started to decline. He still had so much dignity, was still just as noble, just as beautiful, just as majestic. Comet would yelp out in pain when he moved; even going outside was hard for him. Eventually, that spring, we decided to put him in the barn because he had lost control of his bowels. We thought that maybe the sunshine, which he always loved, would help him. Right toward the end, he couldn't even bark, he would try to bark at his pack, but nothing came out.

When we bought our cabin, I thought, sadly, that is somewhere we could lay Comet to rest when it came time. And that first night of summer, we did. I knew when we pulled behind the house, and I didn't see Comet, sitting on his watch, in the doorway of the barn, as if on patrol, that something was wrong. I don't think he suffered in his last moments. He looked as if he had just laid down and gone to sleep. We had prayed that Comet would be able to live long enough for Cole to have memories of him and he did. Right or wrong, we let Cole see him and be with us as we buried him, sitting out in the rain that night, all three of us crying, the rest of the pack sitting on the porch watching solemnly, as if they knew the alpha pack leader was gone. We buried him, wrapped in a blue baby quilt my grandmother had made, feeling he was less alone somehow. When we had put the last bit of earth on his final resting place, we sat there a little bit longer, feeling an emptiness and a void, that has yet to be filled and doubtfully ever will.

The next morning, I remember Cole walking out to the grave, where his daddy was already sitting.

"Tell him to wake up, Daddy," Cole said.

Lamar shook his head. "He's not coming back, Cole. Comet's in heaven now."

Cole's lip quivered a little and he nodded his head, the reality finally sinking in. "He was my best friend, Daddy, in the whole world. My very best friend."

Lamar nodded and said "I know, baby. Mine too."

Me, too.

Where is She?

Phyllis Ellis

The last time I saw her
she was headed out the front door
onto the front porch
where it was sunny and warm.
She stayed out all night,
but she had done that before.
I called out to her at first light,
in hopes that she would hear me.
It was raining and I wondered
where could she possibly be?
I put my coat on and walked around the yard,
looked into the garage where she might be
dry and out of the weather.
I walked down the narrow road
looking into ditches and wooded areas
in search of a possible body.
Where could she be?
Do parents worry about their children like this?
I'm worried.
Yes I'm worried about my cat!

Miss Na'omi Shares Her Aloha

Jill Marie Landis

"So, why not stop at the Kauai Humane Society and just look at the cats while we're in town?"

Just look? Who was I kidding? Myself I guess. I certainly wasn't fooling my husband of forty years. For thirty-four of those years we had cats; sometimes one at a time, but mostly two and then three. Each batch lived to be over sixteen years old. Did you ever notice that once you have a cat word gets out in catdom that you are a soft touch and pretty soon another one has moved in?

Anyway, we went cat-less for six years after moving from the mainland (USA) to Kauai, Hawaii. Our last batch of cats grew very old and after the trauma of finally losing all three we missed them terribly, but we were ready to experience being able to walk out of the house without having to track down cat sitters or worry about little Puff or whoever we left behind.

For a few years all went well in paradise until I found myself staring into the haunting eyes of the cats featured in the photos published in the local paper. Once a week, the Kauai Humane Society runs a "Pet of the Week" article to help get animals adopted out. I remember seeing one photo and actually thinking, "I should call right now." When I finally did call a few days later, a torti named Petunia was already gone. (Adopted I hope.)

Okay, so another year goes by and then out of the blue my husband says, "I really miss having a cat." He looked shocked the minute he said it. He started to go on about how he didn't mean it. He was crazy for thinking it. Life was so much easier. We were free, free, free!

Until we were on the way to town one day soon after and I suggested we stop at the Kauai Humane Society "just to look."

We looked. We looked at all the kittens in the kitten

nursery, a huge room full of cages of adorable kittens. But we've done kittens. We're over kittens. We've had shredded upholstery and mewling in the night, wild rumpuses and strandings in trees. They are precious, but most of them were cuddled up in pairs. I wasn't about to break them up.

We moved on. There were three whole rooms of adult cats. Some were so old we knew we'd definitely be adopting a heart ache if we chose one of the seniors. By the time we walked into the third room, we hadn't lost our hearts to anyone yet. A grey tabby followed us around trying his darnedest to be adorable, but no luck.

Then I saw a beautiful Tortie who completely ignored us because she was fixated on a gecko on the ceiling. She stole my heart. Her name was Na'omi. They listed her as six years old, and I wanted her. Steve thought we'd bring home a Siamese like our previous favorite cat. I reminded him she'd been half Torti and they have "Torti-tude."

We went outside to discuss it. What were we doing? What would it mean to our freewheeling new lifestyle? We sat on a bench in the lobby and hashed it out. The volunteers probably saw us as an old couple on the verge of losing it. You'd have thought we were in China deciding whether or not to adopt a human child.

They reminded us we were getting a three-hundred-dollar value for only fifty dollars! The cat was spayed, microchipped, vaccinated *and* they added, she'd been there three months already so if we wanted her we shouldn't wait. Time was running out.

What? Time was running out? Throw in a carry box and pack up the cat! It was a done deal.

Na'omi didn't let out a peep during the stop at the pet store to get supplies or on the hour ride home. We opened the carry box and let her out in the house. We gave her a tour: "Here's your food in your new ant proof food bowls. Here's your spanking new litter box." She knew exactly what to do. We picked a genius.

We kept her inside for two weeks so she'd know this was "home."

Then we introduced her to her back yard, her own private jungle (which was once full of chameleons and geckos, but the reptile population has been greatly reduced over the last year). An occasional chicken is sometimes foolish enough to wander through trailing baby chicks but for the most part they steer clear now.

Na'omi has made pals with three of the neighbor dogs. She comes when we whistle and sometimes she acts more like a dog than a cat. She follows us from room to room and all over the place outside. She waits for us at the end of the driveway when we go out in the car and she comes in after dinner for TV and bedtime. She has us opening and closing the screen doors on command. She knows all the neighbors and goes calling. They know her by name and have treats waiting.

She has trained us in how to play hide and seek and chase her around the house. Sometimes, not often, she will condescend to sit on our laps but not for more than a couple of minutes. Sometimes she even sleeps on the foot of the bed. It's enough for her to just be close by.

A lap cat Miss Na'omi is not. Not yet anyway. For now she shares her aloha by butting her head against our legs. In the morning she purrs like crazy after she has walked over us long enough to make us get out of bed. We're convinced she's trying to let us know she missed us while we were asleep.

It's been a year since we brought Na'omi home. We

wonder where she lived on Kauai before or if she had any kittens. (She was spayed on entry at the Humane Society). We don't know what her life was like before, but we definitely don't know how we lived without her.

A Radar for Orphans

Sybil Barker

I often describe Dave as the man all the homeless dogs seem to find. I've found only one dog in my life, a husky whom I reunited with its owner the same day. However, for Dave, the neediest dogs have an uncanny sense of being in the right place at the right time to fall into his orbit.

There was the large russet mutt at a BART transit station, whom Dave said would only answer to the name, "Bill Nelson," and that's what he was called the rest of his life as Dave's dog.

Gladys was a chestnut-colored, half-grown pit bull, sitting at the corner of a busy six-lane intersection, when Dave drove by, bringing guests from the airport to his home. After dropping off his friends, Dave returned to find her still sitting there. As soon as he approached, she tried to wag off her stubby tail in excitement, licking his hands and shoes. Dave spent Gladys's first night in his house sleeping on the sofa to keep her company, while she stayed up all night, throwing herself a tennis ball with her mouth and leaping to catch the bounce.

Howard was scavenging beside a dumpster in a large parking lot, when Dave spotted him. His big, tawny body was covered in bite marks, evidence he was used as a fighting dog. Dave sat his tall, lanky self on the pavement to put the stray at ease, then took off his belt to use as a leash. Soon the two of them rode up the rear liftgate of Dave's truck.

It wasn't long before Howard appointed himself the leader of the pack of the five rescued dogs at Dave and Mar-

jorie's house. He was never aggressive with the others; they just seemed to know he was in charge. Howard was friendly with stranger dogs, but when one made menacing growls toward members of Howard's pack, Howard quickly stepped in to make it clear he was their protector. The stranger dog immediately backed off.

Oscar's tale of meeting his destiny as Dave's dog was the most fortuitous. Right after driving away from his house, Dave looked in the rearview mirror just in time to see a car hit a large dog. The car didn't stop, but drove right over the dog, fortunately missing it with its wheels. Dave scrambled up the hill to find a scrawny, stunned shepherd, who struggled to rise when he approached. Dave recognized the dog as one that had been running around the wooded hills of his neighbor

hood for six months, but no one had been able to catch it. Luckily, the injured dog couldn't run away fast enough this time. With a neighbor's help, Dave cornered the dog and lifted it into his car. He drove the animal to a vet, who said there were no major injuries, but the dog's heart had been knocked over six inches due to the impact.

Oscar spent most of the next three years under Dave and Marjorie's bed, too frightened to come out. They even served him his food there. Gladys the pit bull often gave him friendly companionship under the bed. When he did occasionally venture out, and Dave entered the room, Oscar slinked rapidly back to the bed. His rescuer was inextricably entwined in Oscar's memory with the traumatic car accident.

When the household moved, Dave and Marjorie shopped for a new bed, with enough space underneath for Oscar. They couldn't find one, so they made a bed for him in the closet. Surprisingly, Oscar instead took a liking to the top of the new bed, and he didn't run away when Dave sat on the bed. Finally he even let Dave stroke him, cowering at first, then relaxing into it with enjoyment. Oscar even came to revel in daily romps in the park with his canine roommates.

Dave and Marjorie bestowed a longer life of contentment and belonging upon nine abandoned dogs over the years. They found a half dozen more, for whom they ferreted out new homes. When my family prepared to move to a home where we could own a dog, Marjorie told my son, "If you adopt a homeless dog, it will give you so much love! You'll never regret it." Her prediction proved true, when our terrier-dachshund-corgi-and-who-knows-what-else Pogo infused our home with laughter and affection. Marjorie was right: seven years later, we still have no regrets at all. Whatever else is going on in our lives, we know when we get home, there will be an official greeter whose whole body expresses his delight and love.

Just One Live Dog

Bonnie Unnold
(Christmas with Brownie, 1949)

My childhood is not a tale of pets; I had only one real pet, my dog Brownie. He was actually the family dog. He mystically appeared dripping wet one rainy and windy night. We heard something whining on the front porch on Crosby Ave, opened the door and there he was. We had to take him in. I was three and Bobby was five, the perfect ages to have a dog. But Dormont was not the perfect place. With wall-to-wall houses and small back yards, there was no place for a dog to run. I heard my dad repeat, like a mantra, "This is no place for a dog. A dog needs to live out in the country."

So two months before my fourth birthday, we moved out to the country and took Brownie with us. I don't think we moved to the country so Brownie could have a better life, but so we could live in a new house. Still, Brownie benefited. And it was true: a dog did need a place to romp and tall grass to sleuth around in. Our mother constantly warned Bobby and me about the numerous snakes crawling around in the tall grass, so we never went there. But Brownie safely sleuthed there often.

Not long after we became country folk, a meteorological event occurred that we all (especially Brownie) would remember the rest of our lives. It was Thanksgiving Day of 1950. Grandma and Granddad McDonough had come, as always, for dinner. My dad had picked them up at the Pittsburgh bus depot then driven them to our new house. Brownie barked a friendly greeting. As we ate dinner and Grandma sneaked pieces of turkey under the table to Brownie, we looked out of our large picture window and noticed snow falling in large fluffy flakes. It was falling fast and thick. We turned on the television for a forecast. The prediction was for an accumulation of three or more feet of snow, a record amount for our location. This news called for swift and immediate action.

My dad went outside and put snow chains on his tires. My grandparents put on their coats, quickly bade Brownie and us goodbye, and were hustled out the door with a pretend push from my mother. She was hurrying them on their way to help divert a disaster: not my dad and grandparents getting stranded in the snow on

their way to the bus depot, but something worse. Unlike Brownie, who got along with everyone, my mother and grandmother often didn't get along. Being snowed in together could have been a personal disaster causing even more damage to their already fragile relationship. After their departure my mother cleared the table and washed dishes, while Bobby, Brownie, and I watched the snow fall. My dad arrived home before the snow had gotten too deep. Brownie excitedly chased his tail round and round and barked a friendly greeting. My mother just breathed a sigh of relief.

The next morning the snow was about four feet deep. Sun sparkled on this blindingly bright smooth white glistening surface. Bobby and I got snow-suited and snow-booted up for a romp in the snow. Brownie was excitedly jumping up and down and barking. We knew what he wanted, but he was just too little to go out into the deep snow. My dad moved him away from the door, but Brownie was fast and focused. He dashed out the door before anyone could grab him. We watched as the weight of his body broke the crust of the snow, and he dropped like a rock to the solid ground below. "Bark, bark, bark!" We could hear poor Brownie's muffled barking, but we couldn't see him. "Bark, bark, bark . . . whine . . ." My dad retrieved Brownie. He brought him back inside the house and didn't let him go out again to play in the Big Snow of 1950. Brownie stood at our picture window and pressed his wet nose against the glass. Bobby and I waved to him with our snow-encrusted mittens as we built a snowman. Brownie was a little dog—-not big enough to be out in the deep snow even in the country. We hoped he understood.

But snow melts and Brownie was once again outside in his element. Come spring, he was chasing rabbits and sleuthing through tall grass. When summer came, however, Brownie's life was at a turning point. Although he didn't know it, the decision had been made to sell "his" country home and move back to Dormont. We all began to hear that haunting refrain once more: "Dogs don't belong in the city. They need a place in the country where they can run and play."

My parents talked. We couldn't take Brownie back to Dormont with us, but they had an idea. Why not give Brownie to Grandma and Granddad Matthews. They lived out in the country and had a big yard where Brownie could run. Granddad liked to hunt rabbits and squirrels, so maybe he could take Brownie hunting with him. Bobby and I could still play with Brownie at least once a month when we went to visit the grandparents.

Now this is a ploy as old as the hills of Western Pennsylvania: give the beloved family pet to someone else within traveling distance so you no longer have pet-responsibility, but the children can still keep in touch. I once had a baby chick that met a similar fate when it got too big to live in Dormont. Grandma Matthews took it, and I think that I "visited" it one Sunday on my dinner plate. Grandma was known to chase down a chicken in her basement, chop off its little head, cook it, then serve it to the relatives. I knew that this wouldn't be Brownie's fate, but I also knew that I would miss having him at our house. Though not the best solution, it would have to do.

So there was Brownie living in the country with my grandmother, the good cook. Brownie soon found out what a good cook she was, because he got to eat all of the table scraps: pieces of beef, ham and chicken, toast, bacon and scrambled eggs, cakes, pies and cookies. Each time we visited Brownie he looked a little fatter and a little rounder. He began to look like a bloated stuffed sausage about to sizzle and sputter in the frying pan. He moved slower and slower. There was no more chasing of squirrels and rabbits for this fat pup.

My dad became concerned. He was in a dreadful dilemma. If he criticized the way my grandparents were taking care of Brownie, they might become offended and give him back to us, and we all knew that "Dormont is no place for a dog". But if he said nothing, Brownie might die an early death. My dad realized that my grandmother thought she was taking good care of Brownie. After all, everyone else loved her cooking, so why not Brownie? She just couldn't see that she was slowly killing him with kindness and calories.

Not long after my dad became aware of his dilemma, Brownie died. We weren't surprised. We saw it coming. My grandmother didn't. She couldn't for the life of her figure out what had killed Brownie. She talked about having an autopsy done to determine the cause of his death. She never did. Perhaps she concluded that it was one too many cream puffs or chocolate éclairs. We had already figured that out.

Bobby and I knew that we would never have another dog like Brownie or another dog. We knew the mantra by heart, "Dogs don't belong in Dormont", so we knew not to expect another one. Brownie had been a lucky happenstance. He had been our one and only, not our one among many. For that reason alone, we would never forget him.

Banjo

Phyllis Ellis

"I love living in the country. Lots of things to do around here." Banjo said to Molly and Duchess, two ponies grazing just outside the barn.

Banjo, part hound dog, part shepherd and maybe a touch of Doberman, had a long tail and when he was alert, one ear would stand up, the other down.

"Right now, I'm keeping my eye on that lonely chicken that wanders around here. Oh . . . and those cats keep me entertained. When my human friends go for a walk in the woods, that's when I have the most fun. I love running in the woods and chasing squirrels and even deer! Wow, what a life!"

Molly and Duchess could care less about what he had to say. Zara listened. She was a young Arabian filly and wanted to know about everything.

"I can't wait until I can go out into the woods!" Zara said, as she gazed beyond the fenced pasture.

"I bet there's a lot to see out there."

"Banjo, Banjo . . . you want to go for a truck ride?" yelled out an elderly man named Forrest.

"Yeah, yeah," Banjo answered as he ran and hopped in the bed of the truck. His long tail wagged and his part-shepherd, part-who-knows-what, was excited about where he was going.

"I just love riding in a truck, letting my ears fly in the wind!" Banjo was pacing back and forth in the bed of the truck. "What are we hung on, let's go, let's go!"

Forrest started up the truck and off they went into the pasture and then into the woods to get firewood. As Forrest gathered the wood, Banjo ran around the area checking for foxes or squirrels. But Banjo also was keeping his eye out in case that pickup truck was ready to leave.

Sure enough, it was time to go back. "Come on, Banjo, hop in," Forrest said. This time Banjo got to ride in the cab of the truck, since the back of the truck was full of firewood. Forrest drove the truck back to the small barn to unload the firewood. Banjo hopped out of the truck and began his usual routine of sniffing things, making sure nothing strange happened while he was gone.

"Wait . . . I smell something different," as he sniffed the air. "Ah . . . female, yes, female dog!"

He ran up the road, past two or three houses, and there she was, waiting for him. A beautiful St. Bernard dog named Sadie.

"I'm here, I'm here!" barked Banjo, as he ran around Sadie. Banjo was courting her and she accepted him as though they had been lovers all along. She was larger than Banjo, but he didn't seem to mind. Her big beautiful eyes and droopy lips were just, well, "Lovely," Banjo sighed. It was a romantic afternoon until the owners of Sadie came home.

"Git!" yelled the owners. "Git on home!"

They grabbed Sadie and put her back into the fenced yard.

"Git! I said!" yelled the irate man.

Banjo headed home, but he felt good. Love was in the air and he had a wonderful afternoon.

Sadie would escape from her fenced yard now and then, and even visit Banjo at his home. It was a wonderful romance.

One day, Sadie didn't come down to visit, so Banjo went to her home to discover that she had puppies . . . his puppies!

"I'm a father . . . I have puppies that look like ME!" barked Banjo as he started back for home. His mind was on Sadie and HIS family. He wasn't thinking of anything else at that moment. He was so proud of being a father. "Oh, I'm a father! Oh, I'm a daddy to all those cute puppies! PUPPIES! I love puppies!"

Screeeeeeech! Thud!

"Ahhhhhh . . . ooooohhh nooooooo, I've been hit! OOOOOOOOOhhhh, I'm hurt. OOOOOOhhhh!" Banjo yelled out as his body was thrown to the side of the road.

An old pickup truck had hit Banjo. The young man stopped and knew who the dog was and who he belonged to, and ran down the road to tell Forrest and Phyllis what had happened.

"I'm so sorry. I just didn't see him," the driver said with tears in his eyes. "He's still alive, but hurt real bad." He pointed to where Banjo was lying on the side of the road. "We thought we would put him in our truck, but he started growling at us. I think you need to get him. Can I help you with him?" he asked. "Maybe I can help get him into the truck for you."

Forrest, Phyllis and their neighbor, Adele, drove their truck up the road and got out of the truck. Banjo was lying there, and was still conscious.

"OOOOOOOOOOOOOhhhhhhh, I hurt so bad," Banjo

cried. He could see the truck pulling up beside him. "Help me," Banjo cried. "Ohhhh, I can't get up. Ohhhh, what's happened to me?"

Forrest and the young man picked Banjo up and carefully put him in the back of the pickup truck. Phyllis had already notified the veterinarian. Even though it was a Sunday, the vet would meet them at his office. They arrived there in about twenty minutes. The veterinarian slid Banjo on a board and they carried him inside. After a few x-rays, they found he had broken his pelvis.

"There is nothing I can do for your dog," the veterinarian said as he was petting Banjo. "He'll just have to mend on his own. I'll give you some painkillers to keep him comfortable, but he probably will not be able to get up for a while. Only time will tell if he will mend okay."

Banjo was put back into the pickup truck and transported home again.

"Let's put him in the barn," Forrest said. "He won't be able to control his urine and stuff, so it might be better that he be in the barn."

Phyllis and Adele made a comfortable bedding area for Banjo with plenty of blankets and hay to help keep him warm.

"I've got an idea," said Adele. "Why don't I bring Jennifer here to stay with Banjo? She can keep him warm and keep him company."

Jennifer was a young black Labrador puppy, about four months old. She and Banjo didn't know each other that well. She stayed at the house next door and Banjo had been too busy visiting Sadie to pay any attention to young Jennifer.

That evening, the temperature outside was dropping. The weather report mentioned freezing temperatures.

Banjo was shivering.

"Oh, I wish I could stand up. I'm so sore and I can't seem to move around," Banjo cried. "What have I gotten myself into?"

Phyllis slipped an old turtleneck sweater over Banjo's head and pulled it down around his body, pulling his front legs through the sleeves of the sweater.

"Hey, this feels better." Banjo said as he let her comfort him. "Is this why people wear clothes?"

Adele brought Jennifer in and put her next to Banjo. She was shy at first and wondered why she was being put into the barn with Banjo.

"Hey, what are you doing here?" Banjo asked Jennifer.

"I don't know. Your guess is as good as mine." replied Jennifer. "What happened to you?" as she noticed he was injured. She sniffed and realized he had urinated on himself.

"Good grief," Jennifer said, "I'm supposed to sleep with you?"

"I'm sorry," Banjo said softly as he tried to sit up. "I have no control over the situation."

Adele and Phyllis left the barn and turned the light out.

"Don't leave me." Banjo cried out! "Can't I come with you?" The barn door closed.

"I think we're here for the night," said Jennifer as she looked around.

The moon was shining brightly that night. It put strange shadows on the barn. It became quiet as the temperature started dropping, the only sound was of the horses chopping on hay and an occasional mouse scattering across the beams of the barn.

"It really is getting cold," Banjo complained. "I wish I

were inside where it's warm."

"Here, let me snuggle up closer to you," Jennifer said as she put her body up against Banjo's belly. "Isn't that better?" she asked.

Banjo looked at her and smiled. "Thanks."

A week went by and Banjo was able to eat and drink and begin to move his body a little. He still couldn't stand up. He could lift his head and his front part of his body up a little, but the backend was still paralyzed. He was getting bored and impatient with the situation.

"I just don't care anymore," Banjo said to Jennifer. "What kind of life is this going to be? I can't do anything anymore. Here I am a father and I can't even visit my family. I'm so unhappy."

"What should we do?" Phyllis asked Forrest. "It's like he's giving up."

"He's probably bored in here." Forrest said. "What if we get him outside for a breath of fresh air? How about we take him for a truck ride? He loves truck rides."

With that remark, Banjo wagged his tail and tried to get up.

"Yeh, yeh, I'm ready!" Banjo cried out. "Just get me in the truck! TRUCK RIDE!"

Phyllis and Forrest slipped Banjo on to a piece of plywood and put him in the cab of the truck.

"Oh boy, oh boy . . . a truck ride!" he cried as he tried to look out the window.

They started driving down the road, and as they passed Sadie's house, Banjo began to sit up.

"SADIE!" Banjo cried out, "SADIE!" Banjo sat up in the seat of the truck to find out if he could see Sadie anywhere. "SADIE!"

"Look," Phyllis said to Forrest, "he sat up! He's looking

for Sadie."

From then on, Banjo was beginning to get stronger. Weeks went by, and with the help of Jennifer keeping him warm at night and also good company, he was encouraged more and more to get up and even walk again. His back left foot would drag and it became sore from scraping the ground. The veterinarian cleaned the wound up and wrapped his back foot up with tape. He put an Elizabethan collar on him so that he couldn't lick or take the tape off his back foot. When he went to the barn to see the horses, the horses bolted!

"OHHHHHHHH . . . What is that!" squealed Molly. "Run, RUUUUUNNNNNN!"

The horses began to run away from Banjo.

"Wait!" Banjo barked "It's just me!" He ran after the horses, and the more he ran after them, the more they ran from him. "Wait! Wait! I'm not going to hurt you! Wait!"

Finally, the horses slowed down and stopped and stared at Banjo.

"What is that ridiculous thing around your neck?" Molly asked. "You look like a live light shade!"

"Haa haa ha" the horses laughed, as they circled around Banjo.

"Well, I can't help it," Banjo replied as he walked off. "It's supposed to help me with my sore foot."

He looked around and realized he had been running. *He had been running!*

His life was beginning to get back to normal again. He learned to live with a limp, but Banjo was still able to go for walks in the woods and ride in the pickup truck and run with the horses.

Life was good.

Gabe: My Little Answered Prayer

Gina Caufman

My little answered prayer—Being an animal control officer for the last fourteen years, I have saved some lives and I have seen animals lose their lives.

In October of 2006, one of my co-workers placed a carrier of nine abandoned, infant puppies on top of a desk where I was sitting. I refused to peek inside, although I could hear the tiny whimpering of infant puppies. At thirty-seven years of age, a comfortable home and a good bit of knowledge about animals, I thought, "Well maybe I could save just one life." Without looking inside of the carrier, I reached inside and said a prayer. I said, "God, give me the healthiest, smartest puppy in this carrier and no matter what sex or color please don't let it tear up my house!" With that said, I pulled out a darling black and white puppy that I knew would need to be bottle fed.

My life as I knew it changed instantly. The sleepless nights began, but the new found laughter in my home was welcome. I named him Gabriel and called him "GABE." As he grew, and oh boy did he grow, I became more attached to him. My prayer was answered! Gabe was completely potty trained at six weeks. He's smart and handsome. My house is still standing! There is no doubt in my mind that he would give his life for me.

My wonderful Gabe is five years old now and has a two year old little sister named Sydney, also adopted from animal control. Once again my life has changed. Gabe and I say prayers for Sydney each day because we are both convinced that she is ADHD.

Find the Football

Lynda Holmes

My brother hid the football
Last night while we were asleep.
Now that we've finished homework,
We're huddled in a heap.

Whoever finds the football
Will be the champion of the day.
Let's pair up and search
Until it's too dark to play.

Look around the bushes -
Try to find a clue.
Let's think like my brother:
Wonder what he'd do?

Check behind every tree -
Look throughout the yard.
If we seek a solution,
It can't be very hard.

Now that we've been everywhere,
What have we left out?
Instantly, we scamper toward
My pet's austere doghouse.

There lies the football -
The dog is not concerned.
We cheer as, once again,
We've one more lesson learned.

Jamocha
Emily Lewy

Many years ago when my son was little, he was an only child. Although I did all that I could to make sure he had playmates, much of his time was spent alone. This didn't seem like a good thing to me because I had grown up with cats, dogs and lots of family. So I began to talk about getting a dog.

A friend of mine told me about a young couple she knew who had a poodle that they could no longer keep in their apartment. This sounded interesting, so I went to see the dog.

These young folks had made a big mistake getting a cute little poodle puppy that within a very short time grew into a very large standard poodle. They left it closed inside a tiny kitchen all day. Poodles are smart. This one was unintentionally being mistreated and he had become destructive.

Jamocha was a very sweet, very large, beautiful brown poodle. I had a big back yard and I love poodles. Sounded like a match made in heaven. At first it seemed to be.

Jamocha loved the freedom of the big back yard and he enjoyed being inside with us. But I soon learned that if he was left outside alone very long, he would climb the fence.

The area where we lived had too much traffic for a dog to wander around. I installed an electric wire around the top of the whole fence to keep him from trying to climb. But Jamocha was unfazed by the shock. It was not enough to stop a dog that would not be confined.

On two occasions I retrieved him only after running lost dog ads in the newspaper. Very kind people found him, saw the ads and called me. He had traveled miles through traffic. As I say, he was a very smart dog.

From that time on, Jamocha had to be locked inside my house when we were away. Confinement of any kind was unacceptable to him.

He was extremely agile and had no problem jumping onto my kitchen counter tops. On one occasion, he opened the door of an upper cabinet, removed a sealed plastic container of rice, chewed through the container, and ran through the house strewing rice.

I began to consider the possibility that this might not be the right home for Jamocha.

And then I came home one day to find flour strewn throughout my house. He had pulled an unopened bag of flour from the pantry, opened it, and spread it all over the house.

This was too much. I placed an ad in the newspaper, "very large, beautiful brown poodle needs a home in the country where he can roam."

Happily two young ladies answered the ad and took Jamocha to live on their farm way out in the country.

I do hope that Jamocha lived a long happy life roaming the countryside. He had gotten a bad start being adopted by people who were clearly unable to deal with such a large, active dog. Bad habits were his way to deal with frustration.

Jamocha's story shows how important it is to make realistic choices when choosing a pet. A miniature or toy poodle would have been a good choice for the young couple. If his first home had a fenced yard, he might never have become an escape artist. But we do have to accept that there are some very good dogs that just will not be fenced in. The best we can do is find them a home that will be as safe as possible and make sure they don't father any more little escape artists.

Happy Rescue Story: Max, a bulldog, was rescued from a home where he spent his time chained in a yard.

Max asks, "Is this my bed?"

Joey Goes To Hollywood

Joan Gallagher

Joey is a two-year old rescued Silky Terrier who has been part of my life since he was nine months old. As many who met him early-on can attest, he was a "difficult" child. Given up by his original owner, he was yet again relinquished in the summer of 2001, this time to the Boone County Animal Shelter in Kentucky. Luckily, an employee of the Animal Shelter recognized his breeding and contacted a local Silky Terrier aficionado, who agreed to foster Joey while he located a permanent home for him. Just prior to the time Joey was turned in to the Shelter, I had expressed my interest in adopting a silky to train in agility to my girl-

friend who lives in Kentucky. She in turn notified that Silky Terrier owner who was fostering Joey. This conversation chain ended with my airline flight to Cincinnati to rescue Joey and bring him to his permanent home in Northern Virginia, where we were living at the time.

Aware that Joey had probably not received any formal training, I immediately enrolled him in a Basic Obedience class. After repeating two such classes with little success, I enlisted the help of a local well-respected trainer and enrolled Joey in her Saturday morning clicker training class. With her expert assistance and lots of clicker training, distracted, wild untamed little devil Joey emerged into a semi well-behaved and attentive little boy. Joey learned quickly and especially enjoyed learning tricks. Using the clicker, I taught him to sit, down, roll over, play dead, touch a target, jump in a box, sit up and beg, high five, give a paw, and most importantly, a series of tricks that won us a contestant spot on the new Animal Planet TV show, *PetStar*.

Joey and I auditioned for *PetStar* at the World of Pets Second Annual Pet Expo held at the Maryland State Fairgrounds on February 1, 2003. There were so many talented pets auditioning that I was very surprised when the *PetStar* producer called me the following week and asked if Joey and I would come to Hollywood, all expenses paid, that weekend to perform our trick on an episode of the show.

We flew to sunny Hollywood, California, on Friday morning; it was snowing in Virginia as we departed. Joey is small enough to fit into a carry-on pet carrier and has some experience flying, so he was very comfortable during the flight. I was told that there would be another contestant on board the same flight, so I tracked her down.

A representative of *PetStar* greeted us on arrival into Los Angeles Airport. We piled into a van for the trip to the hotel, and although it wasn't the Beverly Ritz, the accommodations were comfortable, clean and pet friendly. Our rehearsal was scheduled for Friday afternoon so we were soon on our way to the CBS Television Studios in Burbank, California. Joey was assigned a dressing room where we both tried to relax until our rehearsal time. The rehearsal went smoothly; it gave us an opportunity to become familiar with the routine of the show, to determine the proper location of our props in relation to the cameras, the studio audience and celebrity judges, and to practice our trick with these distractions. By the time we returned to the hotel, time for a quick dinner was all we had.

Our casting call was set for eight-thirty a.m. on Saturday morning. As we assembled in the hotel courtyard for the drive to the studio, we were joined by some of the other contestants and their pets. The menagerie on our show included an assortment of recognizable breeds of dogs, a bird, a mule and an anteater! Arriving at the CBS studios, we were escorted to the Green Room and assigned dressing rooms. Joey's name was on his dressing room door! Snacks and beverages were provided as we all waited for our chance at stardom. As time passed, contestants became familiar with one another. The producers gave us a pep talk, the contestant appearance order was assigned and the excitement level increased.

Finally, our chance for stardom arrived and Joey and I were escorted from the Green Room to the set. As we waited backstage, I watched the television monitor as pets and their handlers performed their tricks before a live studio audience. The audio man clipped a wireless microphone to my sweater. I gathered up a few treats to have on hand for Joey. Then I heard the show's host, Mario Lopez, announce, "Please welcome Joan Gallagher and her dog, Joey" and the stage curtain opened. As I walked up to Mario, I felt amazingly calm. He proceeded to ask me a few previously rehearsed questions and as I answered them, Joey was quickly becoming a big hit with the studio audience! He barked at a cameraman and was coerced into visiting a few audience members. Joey was very relaxed and comfortable as he trotted around the stage.

Now it was time to do what we came out here to do—his trick! I called him over to me and asked him to sit and stay as I knelt next to his little bench. I directed Joey to turn on his light and he quickly ran over to turn it on. Returning to me, I asked Joey to say his prayers and he knelt down with his paws on the bench and slowly placed his head between his paws. "Ahhhh," emanated from the audience. When I released him from his prayers, he ran to his light to turn it off and quickly scooted to his little house for a good nights' rest. Success! "Joey, the bedtime dog" had wooed the audience. Now, let's see what the three celebrity judges think . . . scores are recorded . . a respectable twenty-five points out of a possible thirty.

Although our scores did not earn us the $2,500 cash prize, I had already won. I got to take home some amazing memories and the best prize of all—a two-year old rescued Silky Terrier named Joey.

(Animal Planet debuted Episode 9 of *PetStar,* in which our segment appeared, on February 28, 2003. It is still being shown in reruns. Joey is now 11 years old and continues to entertain us).

Fur-Ever Feather

Anne Amerson

When our beloved cat Yo-Yo died at the ripe old age of nineteen, I didn't plan to get another cat right away, thinking it would be nice to have some unencumbered time to travel before taking on the responsibility of a new pet. However, our house felt so empty without a furry presence curled up in my lap and sleeping at the foot of our bed, that I soon headed for the local animal shelter.

As I walked into the cat room, a dozen or more felines of various sizes and colors poked their paws through the gaps in the wires of their cages and began meowing loudly, "Take me, take me," or so it sounded to me. I wanted to take them all, but knew I had to select only one. How would I know which was the right one for me and my family?

A white cat named Snow was obviously older and very reserved. In fact, she didn't even leave her perch to come to the door of her cage like the other cats. I wondered if she had been traumatized to make her so withdrawn, and my heart went out to her. However, I wanted a young cat with more life and personality, so I moved on to the next cage.

Next I considered a half-grown male kitten with a beautiful orange coat and strong presence. He pressed his whole body against his cage to get as close to me as he could, purring loudly all the while. It was hard to pass him by, but I wanted a female, so I again moved on to the next cage.

And so it went as I considered each and every cat looking hopefully for a home, most of whom continued to yowl, "Me, me, take me." Then I heard a delicate little voice utter a single hopeful "Mew." Looking to see where it came from, I saw a young calico kitten with a beautiful face to go with her delicate voice. Her markings were an interesting medley of black, gray, and orange set off by a snow-white bib and stockings. "May I hold her?" I asked. When she was handed to me, she fit in the palm of my hand and felt as light as a feather. As it turned out, "Feather" was her name. When she snuggled up to me, purring like a motorboat, I knew she was the one I would take home with me.

When I let Feather out in her new home, her eyes grew wide as she looked around at her new surroundings. At first she was content to stay close to me, preferably in my lap, but as she realized that she was no longer confined in a cage, she gradually grew bolder and began exploring all the interesting new sights and smells. Then she started running at breakneck speed from one end of the house to the other and back again, like a tightly coiled spring that had been released. When she leaped onto the coffee table, kitten and magazines all went sliding and crashed on the floor, but even that mishap didn't slow her down more than a few seconds. When she finally wore herself out, she curled up in a ball and slept soundly for a couple of hours.

As Feather continued to grow, so did her energy level. She climbed up everything she could hook her little claws into (including furniture, window and door screens, and any available leg!) She batted her balls down the hall and chased them down the stairs in the middle of the night. However, her favorite plaything was not a cat toy; it was a make-up brush belonging to my grandson's friend Amanda. Feather was so fascinated by its bristles that Amanda gave her the brush, which Feather continues to carry around in her mouth. When she gets tired of playing with it, she doesn't just leave it lying on the floor; she looks for an empty shoe and deposits it there, to be found later when the owner of the shoe attempts to put it on.

Although she's a furry ball of energy who loves to play much of the time, she also enjoys snuggling up in a lap and being stroked. She's very sociable and, unlike many cats who run from strangers, she makes an appearance to greet everyone who comes to our door. She then interacts with guests by fetching a ball thrown for her or allowing them to pet her. One visitor commented that he

normally didn't care much for cats but that she had more personality than any cat he'd ever seen before.

No matter what Feather is doing at any given time, there hasn't been a dull moment in our household since she came to live with us.

Happy Rescue Story: Daisy, the cat who can sleep anywhere!

Every Little Bit Counts
Elizabeth Curley

When I was sent to Turkey toward the end of the Persian Gulf War (Desert Shield/Desert Storm), my dogs went to stay with my mother for the tour of duty, and my two cats, Sheba and Wayne, went off to Turkey with me. I got a Turkish apartment and the three of us set up housekeeping in rural, eastern Turkey.

My friend and co-worker, Charlotte, lived in a small apartment up the road, with her two cats. Several feral cats hung around her house and one of them had two of the cutest kittens. Charlotte began to feed the whole colony, and eventually decided to capture and tame the kittens. If she succeeded in trapping them, she asked, would I like to have one of the kittens? How could I say no to such a proposition? So, of course, I agreed.

Two things you need to know in advance. Eastern Turkey is mostly rural and cats are considered vermin, not pets. If they eat rats, etc. and survive, all right, but if not . . .

So the cat population is fairly large, mostly sick or starving, and while many kittens are born, few survive to healthy adulthood. The colony that Charlotte fed was among the lucky ones.

It took a few days, but she caught the kittens. She

kept one and named it Texas (her home state). I got the second, a chubby (wormy) gray tabby that I named Biraz, which in Turkish means "Little Bit". He would not be touched, so the next step was rather tricky. First, find a vet—they don't do much small animal practice, so we found a horse vet who was willing to neuter and declaw (front only) and worm the little guys. We took them early in the morning, still in the original cage in which they had been caught, and brought them home that afternoon. As soon as the cage door opened, Biraz was out like a shot, and into the spare room, bandages and all. That was the last I saw of him for the next three months. I knew he was still alive because the bits of bloody bandages were all over the room on the second day, and the food I left out disappeared like magic. But I never saw him.

I came home one day and found him and the other two cats busily playing ball with a large cockroach on the floor. He didn't come to me like the others did, but he didn't run away either.

For the next year, it was a matter of gaining his trust. Little by little, he became easier with me. I was able to touch him, pet him. He slept with the other two. Eventually he allowed me to pick him up.

Then it was time to return to the United States. I only got two pet spaces, so he would ride home in the cage with his buddy, Wayne, while Sheba rode in solitary splendor. He went to the base vet and got his shots and his health certificate, along with Wayne and Sheba. The first part of the trip was on a C-130, where the cats were visible and easily accessible. A brief stop in Ankara, then on the Rhein-Main, Germany. All the kids on the plane checked them out, and, while he didn't come to the front of the cage for petting, he didn't spit and scream, either.

We had a flight change and two day layover in Germany, so all three cats went into the Quarantine Kennel on the Frankfurt side of the airport for a short vacation. When I went to pick them up, the gentleman in charge invited me into the back to catch my cat (an area off limits to customers), as Biraz refused to permit anyone to touch him, and had already scared most of the kennel workers away. I went to the back, opened the cage, and held out me arms. My bad boy came to me right away; and then into the carrier with Wayne. On the transatlantic leg of the trip (a 747), there were lots of vacant seats, so the flight steward offered to check on the babies frequently. He carried tidbits of salmon left over from first class meals—better than the tourist lunch I got!

After a few days at home, I reported to Fort Bragg, NC, and set about finding a place for us to live. Biraz, Wayne and Sheba stayed with my mom in PA for a short time, and there he met the dogs and they became his friends and guardians. Over the next three years we moved to South Carolina, then eventually to Georgia.

His first experience with a vet in Georgia was memorable. The vet insisted that the vet tech hold the cat during his examination and shots— something to do with liability. I tried to explain Biraz' foibles about strangers, but lost the argument. The tech picked him up wearing leather gauntlets. Bir scratched her with his back claws drawing blood from her elbow to her shoulder, then went airborne. The clawless kitty grabbed hold of the top of a cabinet and held on until the vet and tech left the room. He then dropped down and went behind the medicine refrigerator, where he remained for over an hour, thoroughly traumatized. Needless to say, I held him for the exam and shots.

He made friends with my friends. Gay took care of him when I had to go out of town, and he permitted her to pet him. Diane called him the Bir-man. The feral kitten had become a house pet.

Sheba died first, of cancer. Then Wayne, of the same. Biraz was the last to die that year. I think he missed his friends. He spent most of his time snuggled up against the dogs on my bed. Sometimes he would wander around looking for the others. When he died, he left a hole that will never be filled. I have other cats and dogs now (7 cats, 3 dogs). Each has a unique personality, and their personal quirks. But none is as unusual as my Biraz, my "Little Bit" of Turkey.

Martini Anyone?

Susan S. Dodds

My husband and I had four cats and lived in a second story condo in a large city. We had an old, lounge chair that we called THE CAT CHAIR. I had purchased it for four dollars at a rummage sale and our four cats loved it. It needed brushing often and seemed to be always 'hairy'.

We were looking for a church to join since we were new to the community. We visited several. One church in particular had a form for new visitors to fill out . . . name, address, etc. One of us filled it out and left it on a church pew.

One evening our doorbell rang unexpectedly. I pressed the buzzer and a voice said, "I am Reverend so and so from church. Taken aback at the unannounced visit, I pressed the button to allow the man to come inside. As I looked over the stair rail as he ascended the steps, I faintly remembered him from a church we had visited two weeks before. I had no time to clean, dust or (heaven forbid) de-hair THE CAT CHAIR!

Breathing heavily as he climbed the stairs, the Reverend got to our door, shook my hand and pushed past me into the living room. Before I could offer him a seat, he chose his own . . . THE CAT CHAIR. I gulped as I watched his rather hefty frame lower into the chair. I tried not to

"TACO" Tasting the Rev's Martini

stare at his all black suit with the little white clerical collar.

My husband stumbled out of the bedroom in his stocking feet and sat, bewildered on the couch. I asked the Reverend if he would like something to drink. Before I could finish saying "water, coffee or a soft drink", he interrupted with "I'll have a martini . . . never questioning if we had the ingredients to make one." Shocked at his choice of beverage, my husband and I exchanged glances. My husband said, "I just happen to have a little gin and vermouth, but no olives "and hurried to make the drink. Meanwhile the Reverend looked around our living room, saw two of our cats lying in front of the fireplace and remarked, "You have cats, I see. Never cared for cats myself." Choking back my words, I didn't dare tell him that four cats resided in our home." My husband returned with the Reverend's martini and placed it on a lamp table next to THE CAT CHAIR.

For the next thirty minutes, we listened and listened as the Reverend talked and bragged about his naval career, his golf game, his many accomplishments and awards, etc. The two cats that had been lying contentedly by the fireplace got up, yawned, stretched and moved closer to the cat-hating Reverend. Our dear Reverend never once looked at the cats. But, as they crept closer and closer to his chair, he would shoo them away with his foot.

I was getting rather weary of the stories and very upset about the foot kicking at MY CATS in their own home. I was about to muster my courage and speak out, when I noticed our third cat, Taco, jump up on the lamp table with her eyes on the martini. The Reverend did not see her. Taco took a sniff from the martini glass, stuck her tongue in the glass and licked her chin. The Reverend reached down, almost as on cue and picked up the glass for a sip. This little scenario continued for several minutes. Taco would lap at the martini; the Reverend would take a sip. It was all my husband and I could do to keep from laughing out loud.

Finally, after what seemed an eternity, the Reverend stood up to make his exit. As he bade us farewell and turned to go out the door, I gasped. His entire backside was no longer black. From the white clerical collar down to his ankles, the Reverend's black suit was now a hairy mass of yellow, white and gray fur! Well, after all, he did sit in THE CAT CHAIR before I had a chance to steer him away from it. He did insult our cats by saying he did not like cats. We suppressed our emotions until the Reverend's hairy backside disappeared down the stairs.

We closed the door and fell on the floor laughing. Both of us had decided early in the visit that this church and this Reverend were not for us. We wondered amid our giggles what other house calls or official duties the Reverend would have that day before he got home and saw his hairy back side. Much to our relief we never heard from him again!

Gracie

Phyllis Ellis

Long hair, muted colors,
long fluffy tail, with just one
white ring around it.
Eyes yellow, one larger than the other.
A look of mischief in her face.
She really is a "goofy" looking cat.
We call her "Gracie."
Gracie adopted us.
She's not intimidated by
the other cats or dogs.
She moved right in without asking.
With that in mind,
her formal name must be
"Princess Grace."
She goes outside at dusk,
after the birds have gone to bed.
She watches closely for prey,
underneath the front porch.
A mouse, a mole or even a lizard.
She's open for anything creepy crawly.
Hunting is a natural for a feline.
One evening I called for her to come inside.
"Here kitty, kitty, kitty, Gracie!"

She pounced on the porch, with her new found prey,
showing a furry creature in her mouth.
"Meow!" she answered.
The creature jumped out of her mouth
and escaped into the night.
"Where did it go?" As she looked around.
Surprised at what had happened.
She had lost her prey in a matter of seconds,
by letting me know what she had caught,
with a simple responding
"Meow."

Princess & Precious

Emily Lewy

My husband and I first met Princess when she was only a few months old living on my father's farm. The family thought I should take the little thing home with me. But Gerald had never lived with a cat and did not have any desire to do so.

Visiting again a month or so later, I insisted that we bring the cat home with us. We placed the cat in a box lined with papers since we would be driving several hours.

We had been on the road for a while when Princess pooped enveloping the car with a stench that only a cat can create. Gerald, the cat hater, was not a happy man as we continued the trip in a stinky car even after the poop was removed.

A bit further down the road, Princess pooped again. Things were not going well. I had a cat with diarrhea and a husband who was ready to put both of us out of the car. Gerald said, "One more time, and the cat will be left behind!" He was really angry. Princess seemed to get the message and settled in for the rest of the trip.

At the vet's the next day, we found that she had worms. With proper medical care she was soon the most regal of cats and that is when she received the name Princess. I wanted to name her Regina for Gerald's mother; but he still did not like the cat that much.

But in time, Princess won his heart. She purred, she snuggled, and she was a great hunter bringing in anything that moved. On Easter morning, she presented us with a large dead bunny rabbit. Though her hunt sometimes resulted in a dead animal, she often carried in live prey. She brought birds in to fly around inside the house. When Grandmother Regina came to visit, Princess brought a beautiful live bird to her. We did a lot of bird rescue in those days!

Princess was always with me in the garden. On one occasion she leaped ahead of me grabbing a snake from the weeds I was pulling. There were many great snake stories. My next door neighbor who didn't even like cats spent many hours watching the antics of Princess. She alleged that Princess made a game of tossing a snake in the air repeatedly and catching it.

On another visit to the farm a year or so later, we heard the sad story of a mother cat who rejected her two kittens. My sister in law said that she could only care for one and insisted that I take the other. By this time Gerald was beginning to like cats, so we brought Precious home with us.

Princess had a look of absolute horror when she first saw the tiny kitten in our house. I believe she thought we had brought in a rat. It took a while for her to appreciate the little creature.

Precious was only a few weeks old when she came to live with us and had to be fed with a bottle. But once she began to grow, there was no stopping her. Precious soon became the biggest cat we ever had. Every year the vet would say, "If she gains any more weight you will have to put her on a diet."

Precious was a gentle giant. She loved to get behind toads and nudge them to make them jump, but she would never injure a one of them. Princess did not understand a cat that would not hunt.

One of the most amazing sights I have ever seen was Princess trying to get Precious to touch a snake. Princess brought the snake placing it about a foot in front of Precious who looked at Princess and the snake with complete disdain. Over about half an hour, Princess continued gently, insistently pushing the snake ever so much closer to Precious. Finally, Precious used her right paw to quickly touch the snake and then she walked away.

Precious was a lover not a killer. And Princess was just magnificent. My favorite picture of these two has them sitting on each side of the just roasted Thanksgiving turkey. They may have been very different, but on some things they did agree.

Chino The Metal Chimp

Jody Boone Weaver

A loud shrill fills the night, and birds fly away in all directions. The sound of something unpleasant engulfs the silence and is unseen. A muted progression of dark and dismal chords erupts with explosive fury. Chino is busy playing his guitar. One might think that instrument should never produce such music. If so, wrong. Chino loves playing heavy metal music.

Chapter 1

Of all the various an unusually talented animals the Institute For Gifted Animals (I.F.G.A.) has, none is more special than Chino. Poachers in the jungle killed Chino's parents soon after Chino was born. Dr. Karen Larue, a North American zoologist from Alabama, had shot and killed the poachers before they were able to hack Chino to death with their machetes. Dr. Larue was safe only because the government of Zimbabwe protected her.

Because none of the other chimpanzees in the area wanted to adopt baby Chino, he became the official property of Dr. Larue. The president of Zimbabwe signed documents legitimizing the transaction. That night Dr. Larue returned to the USA with the baby chimp.

Chapter 2

From an early age, Chino displayed signs of an interest in music. Dr. Larue played all types and artists to the chimp. Chino tolerated the music that was played, but they weren't his favorites. Dr. Larue had reached her wits' end, when it happened. A coworker of Dr. Larue's, Ted, brought in a CD of a heavy metal rock band that he owned, and started playing it while they ran their tests. The music was loud and raunchy, utterly repulsive to anyone other than metal fans.

"Karen, look." Ted said as he pointed at Chino's cage. Dr. Larue couldn't believe what she saw. Chino was bobbing his head up and down to the tempo of the music. When Dr. Larue would turn the music off, Chino would go bananas. He would turn back flips, scream, and pull on the bars of his cage. However, when she would turn the music back on, Chino would calm down, and resume his head bobbing.

"That is a new one on me." Ted commented. From then on Dr. Larue played metal music while she worked. When her shift was over, Ted performed her duties and continued to play metal music throughout the night, but at a lower volume.

Chapter 3

Chino grew into a healthy adult chimp, and his love for metal music grew with him. As a child, he played along to the music on bongos Dr. Larue had bought him. Chino never missed a beat. Now that Chino was much smarter and much older, Dr. Larue decided to try a new test. Ted played the guitar, and was very good at playing metal music. Upon Dr. Larue's request, Ted brought his guitar and amplifier, and played for Chino.

Chino enjoyed it greatly, and never took his eyes off of Ted's hand movements. What Dr. Larue and Ted didn't realize, was that Chino was memorizing the chords and techniques needed to play metal guitar. One afternoon Chino stuck both of his arms outside of the cage. Ted looked at Chino and Chino pointed at Ted's guitar.

"What does Chino want?" Ted asked.

"I believe that he wants to play your guitar." Dr. Larue replied.

"You can't be serious." Ted protested.

"Yes, let him try." Dr. Larue instructed.

"Okay." Ted said.

Dr. Larue opened Chino's cage and Ted motioned for Chino to come and sit beside him. Chino did as commanded, while Ted detuned the bottom e string on the instrument. Ted handed Chino the guitar, and what happened next was very surprising. Chino strummed the strings openly, and then tuned the bottom e string back to its proper pitch. After strumming the guitar once more to be certain that it was in tune, Chino played every note that Ted had just played. Dr. Larue's and Ted's jaws dropped wide open and they sat speechless.

Never before in the history of the earth had any animal displayed a level of intelligence that Chino just had.

"Man we got one smart chimp here. We could make millions off of him." Ted stated.

Dr. Larue was shocked and angered at Ted's display of mindless capitalism. "No! I can't believe you would even consider that. We've raised Chino from the time that he was a baby!"

Dr. Larue went home for the day following Chino's performance.

Chapter 4

The following day Dr. Larue brought an amplifier and an electric guitar for Chino to have. Dr. Larue unlocked Chino's cage door, and motioned for Chino to come to her. She then made a gesture so that Chino understood that the guitar and amplifier were a gift to him. Chino looked at his gift, and hugged Dr. Larue's neck. She knew that this was Chino's way of saying "Thank you."

A single tear streamed down Dr. Larue's face. Chino saw the tear, and took a finger, and wiped it away. Dr. Larue smiled, and understood that Chino was saying "Don't cry."

Dr. Larue plugged the instrument into the amplifier, and then the amplifier into the wall, and turned on the power. Gino watched every move that she made, and started jamming.

The rest of the day Chino played every note of every metal song that he had heard before, while Dr. Larue attended to her work. Before Dr. Larue went home, Ted came in. Dr. Larue waved goodbye to Chino. Chino stopped playing, waved goodbye to Dr. Larue, and resumed his playing. Ted was still amazed.

Chino plays his guitar every day. Some say wonders never cease.

Scottie
Shirley Fay Smith

Long ago not many people had telephones in their homes. Instead, there was a phone at the lake where all the boats were tied up.

The little family, Mother, Roger, Lorraine, and Troy walked to the lake to use the pay phone. Of course Scottie, the little black terrier dog came along.

The phone call was made and everyone was happy and they all walked home. It was fun to just get out of the house for a little walk down to the lake.

Later in the day we called for the little black dog and there was no Scottie to be found. We asked Aunt Mary and Uncle Mike, the neighbors. We went to the animal shelter, "No Scottie". All the family was sad. Scottie was a sweet little black dog. She was always happy and playful. The family just didn't know what they would do without the sweet dog.

From Monday to the following Monday, Scottie was gone. Early on the following Monday, Mother went outside and who do you think came running up all happy and well fed? Everyone was so happy to have Scottie back. Most likely Scottie must have gotten on a boat for the week. We don't know for sure, but that's what we believe.

Fawn

Key Dismukes

Thirteen years ago someone gave me an unusual kitten, an Oriental with a long, slender body, huge ears, almond-shaped eyes and a tail that is almost prehensile. The color of a young deer, Fawn is like no other cat I've ever owned. He will let no one but me touch him but loves to sit on my lap purring loudly and gazing up at me affectionately. When young he would fetch small objects I threw for him, dragging them back as proudly as any lion with its prey. He was amazingly agile and could jump easily from the floor to a tall bookcase. Whenever I walked across the room he would try to anticipate where I was going and jump halfway across the room to land on my chair or bed and wait expectantly. I have a picture of him turning a backward somersault two feet above the floor in pursuit of a toy I was teasing him with.

When I have been away from home more than a

day Fawn scolds me as I come back through the door in unmistakable cat-speak: Where have you been? I was worried sick; I didn't know if you were alive or dead!

Now Fawn is an old fellow with health problems and walks very slowly. He spends most of his time in his special bed with a heating pad. But he still comes to sit on my lap and purrs happily in spite of whatever discomfort he may have. It may seem strange to talk of a pet as a friend, but I can think of no other word for a creature that has attached himself to me so lovingly.

Happy Rescue Story: Rocky Road went from a local animal shelter to foster care and then to a great home in Florida, where he spends his days on the beach.

Bird-Pal Joey

Ivana Pelnar-Zaiko

"Those mockingbirds are making some racket!" I thought to myself. Not that it was that unusual, what with Cinnamon Patch, our calico cat, right there, trying to get in my way and distract me from weeding the patch of herbs by the back porch. The small bed was tucked away between a large, healthy Catawba rhododendron and a short wooden fence—the favorite perch of many birds, including the couple of mockers that now shrieked and swooped down at me. I decided to shoo off the cat and investigate.

It was not easy to push myself in among the dense, verdant, and twisting branches, to inspect the rhododendron's structure. Sure enough, in the branches just above my head, there was a nest: well, what was left of the nest. The bottom had literally fallen out! One glance at the ground below told the story.

Sitting on the cover of old leaves was a pitifully naked fledgling. Naked and blind he might have been, but also large and feisty—and peeping frantically. Long before, he probably pushed out any siblings. Then, trying to wiggle him-(her?)-self into an optimal position his ambition got the better of him. He pushed right through the nest to a hard landing below.

Mockingbirds are reputedly flimsy nest builders and prefer to steal a ready-made home. My shouting resident pair proved that bad reputation. What to do?

After securing the cat, I went to rummage through a kitchen drawer. You know, the one we all have, where old pieces of string, rubber bands, old corks, and other assorted useful odds and ends find a permanent home. Lo and behold! A saved piece of nylon netting emerged from the messy depth, just the thing with which a nest could be repaired. Combined with four twist ties from the same treasure trove, I was armed for the task. Certainly, I could do better than that mockingbird!

In spite of the parents' continued loud protests, I did just that. After attaching the net snuggly below the broken nest, I added tiny twigs, a bit of hay, and crowned it all with a perfect "pillow-top" of dog and cat hair, which we had always in abundant supply. Carefully, I lifted the now tired-out baby bird and placed it back in the nest. By then, I named him and the tense waiting game began— will the parents return to feed little pal Joey?

The rhododendron bush was not only next to the back porch, but also fronted one of the living-room windows, providing a secret view of the nest. The rest of that Sunday afternoon was spent returning again and again to my observation post. Joey looked hopelessly exhausted and just sat there with his gaping yellow beak dwarfing his entire body.

After a couple of hours of no developments, I felt just terrible. I think I grew even more desperate than Joey. It was just then that I caught movement out of the corner of my eye. Cautiously, mama-bird hopped through the branches ever closer to the nest. Her beak was full of bugs. To my and Joey's great joy, mama-bird's head soon disappeared in his yellow-edged cavern and emerged empty. Pal Joey was getting his supper! From then on, both parents returned to their never-ending task of feeding and catching, catching and feeding.

Watching Joey grow became our favorite pastime—it felt like we gained a third household pet. Remarkably, our cat seemed to sense our protective feelings and did not bother the tree, nest, or birds. We witnessed fuzz turning into feathers, then the vigorous testing of the wings. I am sorry that Joey's first flight happened while I was at work, but my husband found him in the evening sitting quietly in a nearby bridal-wreath spirea. After that, we have not seen our Pal Joey again, but I will never forget him.

My Buddy
Elizabeth Curley

I was living in Jacksonville, Arkansas, with my three cats and my golden retriever mix, Hero. We had a section of the back yard fenced off so that Hero could run outside when I was at work, latched, with a chain run through it, though there was no padlock on the chain. It was mostly to make sure that my Houdini hound couldn't open the gate. I came home one day to find the gate open and the dog gone.

I called everyone I could think of—no one had seen Hero. I made up flyers to post around the neighborhood, offering a small reward. As I was putting up the flyers, a little girl, maybe eight or nine years old, came up to me with a small Chihuahua in her arms, and asked if this was the dog I was looking for. When I explained that my dog was much larger, she asked if I would take this one anyway, because she lived in a trailer park where no pets were allowed, and she had been feeding it parts of her lunch every day. What could I say? I took the dog.

The first stop was to my vet. The poor dog had several infected teeth that had to come out. She had never been spayed and had several tumors on her ovaries. The vet's idea was that she had been kept for breeding, and when she got sick, they dumped her, rather than spend the money on her health care. She needed surgery as soon as possible. I left her there for the works.

After her surgery, I took her home and named her Buddy—don't know why. It just seemed to fit. She had been well-trained, and never left the yard when I took her out. After about a week, Hero showed up all covered with grease and oil. Surprisingly, the two of them got along very well. And the cats took to Buddy as though she were one of them—probably because she was their size and not very antagonistic.

Buddy traveled well. I had a pick-up truck with a cap and a sliding window. Hero would slide the window open and both of them would jump into the front seat, thereby defeating the reason for the cap.

On one trip, we were caught speeding near Memphis, TN. When I opened the window for the officer, little Buddy jumped through the sliding window, and actually startled the policeman. She really acted as though she would attack him—a six-pound attack Chihuahua!

She and Hero were featured in the local paper. They had a section where they asked what part of the paper the reader used the most. I answered that I always cut out the Little Caesar Pizza coupons. I could order the baby pan and the dogs would get two-thirds while I got the other. They sent out a photographer to take pictures of them for the paper, and Little Caesar's sent me a coupon for several free pizzas—which the dogs really approved.

After I had Buddy for about eight months, she started to develop certain symptoms. She became dehydrated and had to be admitted to the Vet Hospital. They kept her there for about a week on an IV, in a cage next to a sick fawn. She was pampered and petted, and I went every day after work to hold her. Over the weekend, the techs took turns spending extra time with her. She died in my arms. I missed her, but I knew that she had fought a good fight and had lived a good life over the previous eight months. I still have the copy of that newspaper feature, and when I think of her, that is what comes to mind.

My Foster Family

Cecile Thompson

My sweet rescue dog, George, didn't like cats. Frankly, I wasn't too fond of them either, never having owned one. I was always highly allergic to them, anyway. Gracie (the middle dog) THOUGHT she didn't like them either.

After George died in August, 2008 we took a chance on adopting Merlin (the cat) and his brother, Arthur (who was hit by a car a month after they came to live with us). Gracie was skeptical and didn't accept Merlin into HER house easily.

Gracie and I missed George so much, and decided it was time to search for a "real" companion. After all, Merlin is just a cat! Despair hit after weeks of searching, leaving shelters empty-handed.

Then I saw Eddie, (whom I named after my late brother) at the shelter, so thin his skin barely draped over his bones. Again, Gracie at first didn't receive Eddie with open paws. But it didn't take long before our family became complete. We all know now that cats are cool!

And I haven't sneezed once!!

A Truly Happy Tale...thanks to a microchip!

Susan S. Dodds

I was doing volunteer work at our local animal shelter one day when I saw the Animal Control truck coming up the drive. I always cringed when I saw that truck because I knew it was bringing one or more animals, in cages, scared and traumatized, who had been picked up somewhere running loose in our county.

This time the truck only housed one animal . . . a beautiful, well fed, white American bulldog. State law in Georgia requires that any animal brought in by animal control or found and brought in by a citizen to a vet clinic or animal shelter must be scanned for a microchip. A microchip is a relatively inexpensive method of identifying a pet. A tiny chip is painlessly inserted into the back of an animal's neck. When a lost pet is scanned with a microchip present, the phone number of the microchip company is displayed on the scanner. A quick call to the company provides the name of the owner and their phone number. Within five minutes our vet tech at the shelter was talking to a near hysterical, elated owner.

The bulldog lived in a loving home south of Atlanta . . . nearly 80 miles from where he was picked up by our animal control officer. He had been missing from his fenced yard for nearly four months. The owner, a young woman, had looked everywhere and finally had resigned herself to the fact that her beloved pet was gone forever.

The young woman drove to our shelter in record time (it's a wonder she did not receive a speeding ticket)! When she burst through the shelter door and her precious "Sam", as it turns out he was named, was brought out from the kennels, it was a sight to behold. The hugging, crying, love and laughter would have brought tears to the most "hard-hearted" person.

So many unanswered questions remain to this day. How did Sam get out of a fenced yard? How did he get 80 miles from home? Who had taken care of him? He was well fed and healthy.

But the most important thing and one we all need to remember; he would never have been reunited with his loving owner had she not cared enough to have him microchipped.

My Life as a Dog (By Susie)

Sandy Steele

It all started innocently enough four years ago when I was just a few months old, playing with my litter mates and doing puppy stuff. Then my owner took me for a ride in his truck to a road by the Chestatee River where it looked like a fun place to swim and scamper through the woods. I wasn't old enough to care about chasing small critters so I just nosed around the grass, and then I saw it: My owner's truck was roaring away and leaving behind a big cloud of dust! I ran as fast as my little puppy legs could carry me, but it was already GONE . . . and I was all alone . . . no litter mates, no friendly voices. What had I done to make my owner so mad? Why didn't he like me anymore? Was it because I had one ear that flopped down instead of standing up like the other one?

I was so sad I just moped along until I saw a house right by the river with a nice man sitting on the porch and a black dog who looked like he would be fun to play with. The nice man held me and soothed my hurt feelings and let me sleep inside his house that night. Things seemed OK for a few days, so I got really scared when the nice man put me in his truck to go for a ride. Was he mad at me too? Where were we going?

But we went to visit his sister, and when she opened her front door I was scooped into her arms all cuddly and soft. She made cooing baby sounds I didn't understand because I'd never heard them before; they reminded me of the kittens at my first house. The cuddly lady called me Susie right away and told me she was "Big Mommy." That first night I slept in her "big" bed right beside her on her "big" pillows, and I hoped I would never have to leave. The next day she gave me little yummy things to eat she called "treats." Then a new curious thing happened: every time Big Mommy looked my way she would smile and start that cooing, baby sound again, usually followed by holding, cuddling, and scrunching her face into mine. Even when I chewed one of her shoes or committed a puppy crime, she laughed and rubbed my ears anyway. It seemed like I made her as happy as she had made me and that I was finally in my FOREVER home.

And now I'm not afraid to ride in a truck any more.

Venus the Storm Tracker

Sudie Crouch

The weather in Georgia can be quite unpredictable at times, like a few weeks ago. On Monday we had snow. That Friday we had tornado warnings and hail. Due to these weather fronts, all the local news channels compete for who has the best Doppler radar, the most comprehensive weather coverage. Whenever bad weather hits North Georgia, my mom, Neenie, calls, all in a tizzy, and the first question she asks is: "How is Venus acting?" Venus is our nine year old female German Shepherd. My husband and I have often joked that she hears voices, is slightly schizophrenic and needs some doggie mental health, but she truly is our weather radar.

Last year when severe storms came through the area, I wasn't worried that we were in immediate danger. Venus stayed close by my side, but never acted like she does when she thinks a storm is imminent. When a storm is really about to hit, Venus will circle around us, like she is getting her herd up, or paw at us, trying to get in someone's lap. She forgets she is seventy-five pounds and not exactly a lap dog. Last night we had some storms move through that must have been serious. Venus burst her way into the bedroom, pawing at us as we tried to sleep, coming up to our faces, panting heavy like a prank caller. If the storm is directly above us, Venus will get up on the bed, digging either us out, or her way in. I can't tell you how many times my husband Lamar has been wakened by her freaking out over thunder, lightning and strong winds, and tried to drag her out of the bedroom so we could maybe sleep. I always argue, why bother, she will dig at the door the rest of the night or until the storm passes.

Venus is not only highly sensitive to storms, but my mom thinks she may be able to pick up on medical issues as well. A few years ago, Neenie had been diagnosed with colon cancer. The day before her surgery, Mom came to visit. Venus sat beside her, sniffed at her stomach on the side where the cancer was, and let out a loud high pitched whine. It turned out Neenie had a severe life threatening infection, not colon cancer. But my momma still swears that Venus could detect the infection. What we had called schizophrenia may have actually been acute perception.

Venus also has a strange phobia about sneezes. When my husband sneezes, Venus goes nuts. She jumps on him as if trying to do chest compressions like CPR. If she can't get to him, she jumps on me.

Before I found out I was pregnant, Venus would nudge the coffee cup out of my hand, like she knew I should not have caffeine. She was even more protective and shadowed me more than usual. Once we found out I was expecting, it all made sense. Venus had known! For two weeks, I had not been able to take two steps without Venus underfoot.

So when the severe spring storms threaten our gorgeous, tranquil North Georgia setting, I do turn on the news to see what they predict. As long as Venus, the storm tracking German Shepherd, is calm, content and not trying to herd us all into the bathroom, I know everything is A-ok.

Smokey

Susan S. Dodds

Home from a long day of teaching I sank wearily into my favorite overstuffed rocker. My three children were playing a game on the living room floor. Our five pets were in their beds or nearby. I must have dozed off for a minute. I was jolted awake by the frightened cry of my 10 year old son, "Mom, there is smoke behind your chair." I jerked my head around just in time to see our black cat, Smokey, urinating on the floor electrical socket. A small plume of smoke was curling up behind her tail. One never knows how one will react in an emergency situation. I am ashamed to say, my reaction was less than adult-like. I screamed hysterically, grabbed the two smaller children and carried them to the front yard. I started grabbing pets and taking them out of the house, all the while, screaming and crying hysterically. As I stood in the front yard, realizing that I was scaring my children and pets to death, I tried to calm down and did a head count. Oh no! My ten year old was missing. As I rushed back in to get him, he appeared in the open front door, calm, cool and collected. "Mom, I called the fire department and I called Dad at work. Don't worry, they are on the way."

Shamefacedly, I heard sirens in the distance and realized that my amazing ten-year-old son had done what an adult should have thought to do. What a kid!

As the large hook and ladder pulled up to the front of the house and four firemen in all their regalia went running through my front door, I followed and pointed out the rather large cloud of smoke now filtering out of my floor electrical socket. Two of the men ran to my basement stairs. One had a fire extinguisher in his hands, the other, a hatchet. My heart stopped when I saw the hatchet. I pleaded with the chief to "please" not let his men chop my house up! They emerged about 10 minutes later. They reported that an electrical fire had started in the ceiling of the basement directly under the floor socket. They had not had to use the hatchet and were able to safely extinguish the flames with the fire extinguisher. I breathed a sigh of relief.

The fire chief told me he needed to make a report and asked me to sit down. Checking on the children I saw that they were in good hands being entertained by my very capable ten year old.

"What do you think started the fire"? asked the fire chief.

I took a deep breath, realizing that the moment of truth had arrived and that I could not wiggle out of telling what really had happened. "My cat peed on the socket and smoke came out of the opening." I detected a slight twinge at the corners of the chief's mouth.

To this day I am not sure if the chief was trying to teach me a lesson or show me for the fool I had been. "Could you describe this cat for me? And by the way, it's lucky it wasn't electrocuted." he said, pen poised in midair.

"Well, she is a long haired, black cat." I answered timidly.

Leaning toward me, and definitely 'playing me' at this

point, he asked, "And what is her name?"

Wincing with embarrassment, I answered, "Smokey."

As if on cue, Smokey the cat appeared in the open door and tail erect, pranced between the chief and myself. I suddenly heard guffawing and turned to see that two of the firemen who had been behind me, listening, could contain themselves no longer. As I turned back toward the chief, he too was laughing. I glanced over toward Smokey. Just as I did, that darned cat turned her head slightly toward me, meowed and trotted off to the food dish.

Realizing that I deserved to be the butt of a joke I also smiled. Before leaving the house, the chief gave me some good advice. "Ma'am, I suggest you go to the nearest hardware store and get some electrical socket covers so that Smokey won't be tempted to start another fire."

I'm Nothing But a Hound Dog

Phyllis Ellis

I've been abandoned and I don't know where to go.
I wander the streets in town and neighborhoods,
for someone I might know.
I'm hungry and searching for food.
Being lonely and desperate,
isn't helping my mood.
I need a comfortable place to sleep.
Warm, dry and safe
for more than just a week.
I need someone to adopt me,
and I'll give you love.
You'll see.

What A Dog Will Never Know

Shay Gravitt

Thursday evening around seven-thirty, my uncle walked in with the prettiest dog I have ever laid eyes on. You could tell she was scared. Tail tucked between her legs, ears laid back, eyes alert, sniffing the air. My uncle looked at me and said, "I know it has only been four days Shay, but I figured you might want someone new. She will never take the place of your Quivers, but I hope she will help fill a new hole." With that he let her go. She ran for it. Straight up the stairs into my room. I followed. She wouldn't come out from under my bed until that night. Little did I know that this dog was going to take me on a marvelous journey.

My name is Shay Gravitt and at the ripe old age of fifteen, my house burned to the ground. It was Sunday, December 12, 2010. I will never forget that day as long as I live. Our church was holding our annual Christmas play, and I was in it. My best friend was coming to the play, too. Before we left for the play that night I lit our kerosene heater. She looked back before we left and I will never forget the look on her face. "Is that thing smoking?" I passed it off as nothing since it always smoked when you lit it. We left in a hurry since we were late. That play was one to remember. There was the testimony of many people all over the church. But I knew something was wrong. My aunt and uncle were in the back, and they both got up at the same time and went outside. I just hung my head, sad, that we meant so little to them. Not even thirty seconds later though, my uncle came bursting through the back door running. "I don't mean to interrupt you preacher; but one of our houses is on fire and we have to go."

My whole McKinzey side of the family lived on one hill. There were three houses within a stone's throw of each other. Everyone that lived on that hill was in that church that night. We all grabbed a kid and ran. We left too, and I knew when I climbed into the car that it was our house. I felt a calmness edge its way into me not to cry yet, that I had to be the strong one. We flew down the road going no less than ninety the whole way. My mom and little sister beat us there. My best friend was in the middle of the car and my oldest sister on her right. My phone rang and it showed my little sister's name. "It's gone Shay! Our house is gone!" Her screech is forever etched in my mind. I could hear the fire roaring and see it over the hill as she screeched those agonizing words so loud that everyone in the car could hear. I hung up as we slid sideways into our road. The night was orange with fire.

I only looked once. The fire was so bright. I watched the last wall of the house fall, the wall to my bedroom. It's kind of ironic now though. The last room to fall, the last to break down. In that house were the most precious animals ever. Trixie, Esther, Peanut, Rosie, 3 kittens, Flash, and my Quivers. We thought at the time that Boo-Boo was in the house but he had escaped somehow. I stood strong and tall and didn't think about it till later. It took my dad three days to get home and the day that he got home we were already in a new house.

What little stuff we had sat in the living room as my uncle came in that Thursday. He brought with him the most precious gift I could ever have. My real best friend. Molly Ann Gravitt sleeps at my feet every night. She has the prettiest butterscotch color fur, with eyes to match. My savior lies within the body of a dog. My Molly.

I didn't break down until I was buying shoes and I realized that I never would be able to watch my Quivers jump around again. I broke down crying that night and Molly crawled up in my bed ever so slowly and licked each tear off my face as it rolled down. It was almost like she grieved with me. She sits here in my lap now and sleeps like a little angel. Her story really begins with the end of one of my dogs. She was a savior that never knew it. She stayed by my side through everything. Every time I cried she was there for me to hold. My little teddy bear with a heartbeat. Who knew such a little dog could change a person so much? My mom told me that from the first day she knew the dog loved me the most and it is so obvious now. I'm her everything and vice versa. My little butterscotch will never know what she means to me. I just hope that someday everyone will have an experience like I do with my dog. It's not something I see often though. But I would die without her. I never give her enough credit. This is one of the only ways to give her credit though. Through a story that everyone else can read.

IN LOVING MEMORY OF QUIVERS, THE LITTLE CHIHUAHUA THAT WORMED HER WAY INTO MY HEART AND IN RESPECT TO THE ONE THING I COULD NEVER LIVE WITHOUT

The Day Tony Came Home

Mary Ellen Moore

As dogs go, I am a fairly handsome collie—young, male, obedient and very much loved. Of course, I'm a lover too, and I love HER very much and all the people who visit HER, especially the children. I have a great yard to play in, and I never leave it unless SHE walks down the street; then I'll walk too, and we get some exercise. We both enjoy seeing people and visiting with the neighbor. I've lived with HER a very long time, and SHE brushes me and talks to me and feeds me good food.

One day something happened: I really don't know what exactly, but I wasn't living with HER any more, and I was afraid and confused. I had a rope around my neck, and I couldn't run. Then I was in some kind of cage for a long time. I didn't see any people who loved me, and no one would feed me. I was hungry and thirsty and my coat needed brushing. A long time passed, and I wanted to get home.

Some people came and let me out of the cage, but they didn't brush or feed me, and I could tell they didn't love me. They tied the rope to something, and I couldn't move very far. I wanted to go home.

I started chewing the rope. A long, long time passed. I tried to dig, I chewed the rope, and I dug more and more every day. I know SHE was looking for me and needed me.

I chewed and dug every day and every night. It was a long, long time. One morning, the rope broke, and the digging had made a hole for me to get through. I ran and ran and ran. I wasn't sure which way to go to find HER, but I ran and ran anyway.

A long time passed, and I was very tired and hungry and sad. I went across this road and that road and got into some mud and briars, but I kept trying to find my way. A long time passed. Would I ever get back to HER? I kept running.

Just as I was resting for a few minutes, I looked up and saw something I knew. Even though my paws hurt, I ran faster and faster.

At last I was home! I was back where I belonged. SHE was as happy to see me as I was to see HER, and all the other people came to see me too, including the children. They were all loving me and brushing me, giving me food and water and putting medicine on my feet. I was so happy to be home that I licked their hands and faces to tell them how glad I was to see them.

Postscript: Tony was a two-year-old collie who had been living with my great-grandmother since he was a puppy. When he disappeared, she was heart-broken and searched for him for months. Then one day Tony, unbelievably, found his way back. His coat was matted and dirty, his pads were bleeding, and a piece of chewed rope was still tied around his neck, but he found his way home. He lived many more happy years, loving life with all the people who loved him.

Tinkle, Tinkle Little Cat . . . or Bathroom Humor

Susan S. Dodds

Puddy LeRoy came to us, as have most of our pets over the years, as a stray kitten . . . hungry, skinny and dirty. A cute little ball of fur, he decided quickly that he liked the food, enjoyed the soft beds and could tolerate the other 6 pets who lived in our home.

One night (after Puddy had been with us for about 8 months) I was awakened from a sound sleep by the sound of someone urinating in our bathroom, which was located directly off the bedroom. The door was slightly open and I could see that the night-light in the bathroom was on. Assuming that my dear husband had made a foray to the commode, I started to drift back to sleep. As I stretched, my hand touched something soft and warm on the other side of the bed. Jolting upright in bed I realized with a cold chill that my husband was snoring softly next to me and was not in the bathroom! I shook my husband awake at the same time whispering, "Shhh, there is a burglar in our house and he is peeing in the bathroom!" Still groggy from sleep, my husband sat up, also. I reached for a lamp or something to throw at the burglar as he emerged from the bathroom. Just as my hand touched the lamp I saw a shadow emerge through the small opening in the door. My hand flew to the lamp switch instead of grabbing it to throw. There in the bright light stood Puddy LeRoy, blinking in the sudden bright light, tail erect and with what appeared to me to be a smug smile on his face. I rushed into the bathroom and peered into the commode. Yes, my wildest thought was true! Puddy LeRoy had just peed in the toilet!

How? Why? All sorts of questions filled our conversation for most of the rest of the night. We could not sleep for the laughter at such a sight, the adrenalin rush of thinking we had to deal with a home invader; and the mystery of how that little cat had learned to potty-train himself filled our minds.

Puddy only survived another year before being untimely taken from us by a mysterious illness. But, during that time I twice saw him emerge from our bathroom, tail erect, smug look on his little whiskered face. As my husband and I have said millions of times, "If only animals could talk!"

Happy Rescue Story: Coby. Dawn Chappelle got Coby from a Florida humane society. It's easy to see that Coby's journey from homeless to having a good home didn't daunt her sense of humor.

Coby:

Dawn Chappelle

Dear Staff,

Just wanted to give you an update on our adoption.

From the records we received, it looked like the dog came to your facility in January 98 and was adopted by a family sometime between January and April. She was returned on April 27, 1998, for chewing, digging and hyper behavior. We visited the shelter on May 1 in a completely heartbroken state. We had lost our beloved Sandy to cancer 1 week prior. The week had been awful. We were filled with sorrow and the tears wouldn't stop. We both felt a horrible emptiness in our hearts. We knew we needed a dog to heal our hearts and stop the pain.

My husband and I didn't talk about what type of dog we were looking for, just went looking. We ended up in different areas of the facility, he looked at puppies and I looked at adults. Gypsy, as she was known then, licked my hand through the fence and I knew she was the one for (me) us. After a brief visit with the 1 - 2 year old black, lab mix weighing about 70 pounds, we went to the office to complete the adoption paperwork. As I recall, the two ladies in the office questioned us about leaving the dog alone during the day. Since we both worked, there was really no choice. The women were hesitant to allow us to adopt and I had to promise that I would drive home each day at lunch and take the dog out. Which by the way, I did faithfully for the first month until Coby acclimated to her new home.

Coby has accompanied us on almost all of our vacations, from the mountains to the seashore. She learned complicated tasks such as getting my shoes to go for a walk. She learned how to retrieve her food dish at meal times and any other time she wanted a snack. We now live in the mountains and no longer have jobs. She has enjoyed the wide open spaces and our daily companionship.

Many months and years have gone by since that fateful day she came into our lives. As you have guessed by now, Coby is a very senior dog, somewhere between 13 and 14 years old. She has poor vision due to cataracts, major hearing loss and hips that barely hold her up. She still gets around but most of her time is spent lying at my feet when I'm home and looking out the window if I'm gone. She has been my most loyal and devoted friend for the past 12 years. The bond we have runs deep and she is truly a one in a million dog.

As Coby's life draws nearer to the end, I felt the need to write about this wonderful dog and share her story with the organization responsible for her salvation. Thank you for taking her in. Thank you for allowing us to adopt her and give her the wonderful life she so truly deserved. She is a good dog, a great dog, the best dog!!

Thrown Away

Gloria S. Niles

The word Thrownaway is my term for dogs and cats whose owners no longer want them, put them in a car to be driven—not to an animal shelter—but to any place away from home and tossed, without thought that the pet will probably die of starvation, be killed on the road or become coyote dinner.

Occasionally a thrown away will be found and rescued...

PATCHES

December 1971

To be honest, I didn't pay much attention to my 10-year-old daughter, Amy, when she told me she was sharing her lunch with a puppy on the schoolyard. At that time there was no school cafeteria—the children ate their lunches from home outside near the playground. I did pay attention when she asked about bringing the puppy home.

Since we had two dogs, a cat and a parakeet—not to mention an aquarium full of fish—I wasn't too keen on the idea of another dog. However, when asked what she wanted for Christmas, her only wish was for the school-yard puppy.

So...

On the drive to the school, I was told the puppy's name was Patches because he looked like his mother had made him with what was left over after making other puppies.

I was in for a shock. I expected to see a typical puppy, fat and playful. What I saw was a skinny weak little dog. There was no way I could take him home without a veterinarian's okay.

Driving directly to our vet's office, I left child and dog in the car while I hurriedly explained the situation to the receptionist who asked me to wait in the car while she told the doctor. I waited, wondering how to prepare my child for the probable death sentence.

The vet was upset by the puppy's condition . . . And I was glad we were clients of his and he knew us as people who took care of their pets. But after a thorough exam, he was able to tell us that the puppy was probably mostly fox terrier, about four months old and ended by saying, "If this puppy ever had worms, they starved to death."

Severe malnutrition was all that was wrong—even the hair loss was caused by lack of nutrition. After writing out a special diet, he told Amy to feed Patches 2 tablespoons every three hours for two days, then start dog food. He told her the puppy must be kept on a soft blanket or pillow with a piece of towel or blanket over him to keep him warm—especially at night.

That night when I peeked into her room there they were. Dog bed ignored. Patches was in her bed, covers up to his neck, his head on the pillow and she, the same, with her hands resting on her puppy. This was to be their routine throughout his life.

The following summer, the recreation center had dog obedience classes. On the first night there were about 20 adults with various breeds of dogs and one young person, Amy, who was very nervous. And Patches, who was very excited. Ever anxious to please Amy, Patches quickly learned the basic obedience—sit, come, stay, down, but he just plain didn't like to heel. He preferred a step or two in front—not pulling or tugging—just walking quietly in front. There came a time, in his middle years, that this preference saved Amy. While they were taking a walk in the woods, Patches in front, he suddenly stopped and turned sideways, preventing her from taking a step. A yard ahead of them was a good-sized copperhead snake whose color blended in with the red soil. Girl and dog retreated. Presumably, the snake went on its way.

Patches was seven years old when the accident occurred. Amy and Patches were in the front yard when he saw another dog on the other side of the busy two lane road in front of the house. He took off running and barking. For the first time ever he ignored her command to come and ran onto the road without attention to all the traffic. The driver couldn't avoid him. Patches rolled, then ran into the nearby woods. Since I was at work, the first I knew about it was a hysterical phone call from Amy ending with the fact that she couldn't find him. Finally she calmed enough to listen and I convinced her that Patches would want to be with her, but she must sound calm and caring. She did find him hiding under a bush. Her brother drove him to the vet clinic where he was soon in surgery. Patches lost his right rear leg and a white tip on the end of his tail.

His recovery was remarkable. It was almost as though he told himself, "Oh well, I'm down to three legs. Let's get on with living." Within two days of the surgery he was going up and down the porch steps. By the fourth or fifth day he was wanting to play with the ball. It took a little longer to chase a Frisbee.

The years rolled by. The girl became a young woman, working as a veterinary assistant; Patches slowed down, showing some signs of aging, but the love and devotion between them remained strong. Patches was eighteen years old when his heart failed and he left us. We still miss him, this Thrownaway puppy who wanted nothing more than to love and be loved.

GRETA

Winter 1982

Greta was found in a city park on a cold wintry day, desperately trying to keep her newborn puppies warm amid ice covered leaves. Three of the puppies were dead. The fourth died within an hour. This little black and tan dachshund soon warmed up but it was obvious that she was not only a Thrownaway but she had been abused. She was fearful of everything—a sudden noise such as a knocked over glass; anything in my hands such as a magazine or newspaper sent her crying through the house and as far under the bed as she could get. She did respond well to gentle handling and within a week or so was comfortable in her new home . . . except for her fear of screen doors.

Greta was with us for eleven years and not once did she go outside, past a screened door without stopping, eying it, before racing past it. Didn't take much guessing to know she'd been slammed by one more than once.

The love and trust of this little Thrownaway dachshund will always be remembered.

BRANDY

1992

By this time, Amy was married, living near my house, still working as a vet assistant. I was busy weeding the kitchen garden when Amy walked over, a lovely golden retriever on lead. She told me what happened. A man she barely knew at the feed store had called her in an extremely angered state and told her she'd better come get this dog or he was going to kill it. Of course, she went. It was soon clear to her that this man knew next to nothing about dog behavior, wants or needs. It seems the man chained the dog to his front porch while he and his wife went to work. When they came home eight or nine hours later, they found she had chewed on the steps, railing and ruined a pipe under the house. Since the man didn't want to hear reason, Amy brought the dog home to me.

Brandy became my constant companion. No matter where I was, or what I was doing, she was there . . . unless I was mowing the yard. She hated that mower. On mowing days, she elected to sit way off on the side, watching my every move. Not until the mower was quiet and put in storage did she come near me.

Even good things come to an end. Brandy was with me more than 14 years—always the companion, the comforter and a true friend. For weeks after she was gone it seemed as though I could feel her near me. I felt surprised when she wasn't visible. Time does heal.

WALTER

1994

Amy was still a vet assistant when Walter was brought to the vet clinic to be humanely 'put down'. A hiker had found the blonde, purebred cocker spaniel in a remote area of the North Georgia mountains in such bad condition that he thought it best to simply have him "put to sleep". However, as the vet, with hypodermic needle in her hand, looked at him, there was just something about him that stayed her hand. He sat as upright as a cadet, making no attempt to run, didn't snarl or try to bite. Just sat there with big brown eyes looking at her steadily. She decided he was worth trying to save.Examination proved him to be basically well, just starving. She guessed his age to be four or five years and he weighed only seventeen pounds instead of the usual thirty-something cockers should weigh, with ribs and hip bones jutting through severely matted fur, which was full of ticks and fleas. So, instead of going into a permanent sleep, he was sent back to the groomer where he was shaved, practically to the skin, bathed and dipped until he was vermin-free and started on a diet meant to get his tummy used to food again.

I forget why I went to the clinic that day, but when I got there, all the girls were talking about the cocker spaniel. Amy took me to the cage rooms. I could see him and I fell in love. I had to have this dog. Having recently lost the Thrownaway, Greta, as well as my little purchased Maltese—both to old age—I had room for him.

A week later, the cocker, now known as Walter, came to his new home with me. At first, I thought his desire to stay in the pet taxi, even though the door was open, was simply that he felt secure there after his lonely, frightening time in the forest, but he wouldn't come out to eat, had to be carried outside to take care of his "bathroom" needs.

Once outside, his behavior was unnatural in that, placed on the ground, he promptly lifted his leg, then waited to be carried back inside. No sniffing around or multiple leg-lifting. Days went by. I tried putting his food bowl a little further away from the cage to encourage him out and he would come out, gulp down the food, then literally leap back into the taxi. I was greatly discouraged. I decided perhaps a leash would help. Maybe he would walk outside on the leash. He didn't seem to mind the collar but one look at the leash sent him cowering as far back in the taxi as he could cram himself. Amy and I had come to the conclusion that his dependency on a box was not due to his days (weeks) in the forest, but due to his life before the forest. He seemed to know nothing about dog toys or a ball, ignored the other dogs—his behavior was just unnatural and we felt that he had spent his years in a box or cage, perhaps as a puppy mill's stud dog.

Just as I was most discouraged, unable to think how best to get him over wanting to be caged, a friend of a friend called me wanting to know if I could give a home to a twelve-week-old Cocker puppy who had been born with heart problems, couldn't be sold and she had to go out of town. With some apprehension, I said "Yes".

Blonde like Walter, she became Walter's teacher, his life saver. We called her Annie. The first couple of days Walter stayed in his box watching Annie romp and play. Then, one night after the other dogs were sleeping, Walter crept—on his belly—out of the box, back to the wall, slowly, very slowly on his belly he inched his way along the wall, watching me. I pretended to still be reading but watched him out of the corner of my eye. He moved along the wall until he reached the corner, then curled himself into as small a ball as possible, still watching me. Moving slowly, I went to him, petted and praised him for being such a good dog. He was still there when I went to bed, but in the morning he was back in his box. The next day was the same, watching Annie from his box, belly-creeping to the corner at night.

Third day. The same, except he didn't go to the corner. He came and put his head on my knee! Words fail to express the joy and pleasure that was!

From then on, things improved. It was Annie he followed as he walked outside to the yard. It was Annie he imitated when he began to sniff around the yard. It was Annie he sat next to when he finished eating. He seemed fascinated by Annie playing with toys or balls but he made no attempt to play. Never did.

Annie was five years old when she came down with pneumonia which failed to respond to antibiotics. Unable to breathe lying down, she had to be held in a sitting position. Hour after hour I sat with her, Walter beside me. The first time, he gave her a friendly lick. However, her ailing heart couldn't take the strain and she went to sleep for the last time.

Of course Walter missed her, and I was afraid he would go back to his old ways. He never looked for her. In his own doggie way he must've known she was gone, and life went on. He continued to develop more normal doggie ways, but he never played.

Walter was about fourteen years old when he joined Annie in a final sleep—heart failure. He was a Thrownaway who taught me as much as I taught him.

BEANIE

Winter 1994 or so

It was pouring rain and very chilly when someone brought a young tabby kitty to the vet clinic. She was soaking wet, almost comatose from the cold air, with a Beanie Weenie can stuck on her head. Once the Beanie Weenie can was removed, she was wrapped in warm towels. Naturally she was referred to as the Beanie Weenie Cat, soon shortened to Beanie, thus she was named.

I don't remember how Beanie ended up as part of our family, but she was the first and only cat I've ever had that liked to play "fetch". It was purely by accident that I discovered this trait, when I threw a wad of paper to the wastebasket and missed. Beanie pounced on it, brought it over to me and dropped it at my feet. Curious, I tossed it again and again she brought it back and dropped it. When she was in the mood, she enjoyed this activity; if she wasn't, she would stare icily at me as though it was beneath her dignity to pick up a wad of paper.

Beanie is at least in her mid-teens now, lives with Amy, but never sticks her head in a can. She enjoys her food in a dish, basking in the sun and, occasionally, playing fetch. She's one very lucky Thrownaway, as she could have died beside the road with a Beanie Weenie can on her head.

PIXIE

Spring 2011

And there is Pixie, found by a lake in North Georgia, she . . . But her story is just beginning.

These lucky Thrownaways are among the very few.

Most die, one way or another, because they are domestic—people dependent—animals; thousands of years away from their ancestors who were wild animals. If only people would be aware that it was mankind who bred the wild instincts out of cats and dogs, we would have far fewer Thrownaways.

In memory of Gigi, Cleo, Moe, and Uma